BUILDING
screened
rooms

By Don Vandervort and the Editors of Sunset Books, Menlo Park, California

SUNSET BOOKS

VP and General Manager: Richard A. Smeby
VP and Editorial Director: Bob Doyle
Production Director: Lory Day
Director of Operations: Rosann Sutherland
Retail Sales Development Manager: Linda Barker
Executive Editor: Bridget Biscotti Bradley
Art Director: Vasken Guiragossian

Building Screened Rooms was produced
in conjunction with HomeTips, Inc.

Editor: Don Vandervort
Managing Editor: Louise Damberg
Assistant Editor: Gabe Vandervort
Principal Illustrator: Bill Oetinger
Additional Illustrations: Jim Kopp
Graphic Designer: Dan Nadeau
Contributing Editors: Scott Fitzgerrell,
    Patricia Freeman
Production Coordinator: Danielle Javier
Proofreader: Kristinha Anding
Editorial Assistant: Kit Vandervort
Index: Rick Hurd, Rick's Indexing

contents

SOUTHERN CHARM
Decorated and furnished in classic country style, this screened patio creates a comfortable and colorful open-air living area with an expansive view of the outdoors.

screened retreats

IMAGINE YOURSELF RELAXING IN YOUR BACKYARD ON A balmy summer evening. You're about to enjoy a pleasant meal on your patio when—BZZZZZZZZZT!—a swarm of yellow jackets descends on your dinner while a squadron of mosquitoes goes straight for your ankles. ■ Now picture the same scene, but add a screened room. In addition to protecting you from pesky insects (and the potentially deadly diseases they can carry), a screened-in room can provide filtered shade on hot days, and—one with a solid roof—can keep you dry in a thunderstorm. It can increase your privacy, bring light and air into your house, and offer a nostalgic alternative to central air conditioning. Reclaiming outdoor space with a screened room is also a very affordable way to expand your living area and add value to your home. ■ Today, the universe of screened structures includes patios, decks, pool and spa enclosures, sleeping porches, gazebos, and garden rooms as well as updated versions of the traditional screened porch. Following is a closer look at examples of these screened retreats and how they can make your home more enjoyable and bug-free.

classic screened porches

Popular for generations, screened porches have made a major comeback as a stylish and effective barrier in the battle against bugs.

A screened porch brings to mind idyllic images of a time when people spent long summer evenings on the veranda, visiting with neighbors and watching fireflies flicker across the lawn. Screened porches were ubiquitous in many parts of America in those pre-air-conditioner days. Now these old-fashioned icons of summertime are being rediscovered as a charming way to enjoy outdoor living without insects.

If your house already has a porch, you're blessed with the simplest of situations for creating a screened room. You won't have to build a foundation, floor, or roof—the most difficult and expensive tasks you would face if you built a new structure. All that's necessary is to affix screening to the posts on your porch. A do-it-yourselfer with basic skills and standard tools can complete the project within a few days. Because no major construction is required, enclosing a porch is a very affordable way to expand your living space.

Another advantage of working with an existing structure is that the major decisions have already been made: There's no need to figure out where to put your

▲ *COUNTRY STYLE*
A natural-wood house-wide screened porch harmonizes with the surrounding woodsy landscape.

▶ *LAKESIDE OASIS*
Wide screened bays open this dining porch to expansive views and cool breezes without the bugs.

◀ **RUSTIC BREEZEWAY**
Screened panels attach to the lodge-pole construction of this country porch.

▼ **BEACH RETREAT**
Floor-to-ceiling screens protect this open-air beachside room, yet allow a seamless connection with the sea.

screened room, how big it should be, or how to make it blend with the architecture of your house. Your task will be simply to determine what kind of screening you want and how you'll attach it.

Though your workload is limited, your design options are legion. You can stick with a popular low-cost screening such as aluminum or fiberglass, or choose copper, brass, or bronze for durability and nostalgic appeal. You can even find specialty products that block sunlight or resist shredding. For more about the various types of screening available, see page 90. Affixing the screening to your porch is a snap, as discussed on page 40. By the end of a long weekend, you'll be able to enjoy a bug-free bit of yesteryear.

7

screened patios and decks

If you have an existing patio or deck, adding screened walls and a roof can transform the space into an alluring outdoor retreat.

Patios and decks set the stage for summertime living at its casual best. Add screened walls and a roof, and you create a sublime new indoor/outdoor space where you can relax, dine, or entertain even when the weather is drizzly or the mosquitoes are on the prowl.

An existing patio or deck gives you a head start when you're building a screened room. The relationship between your outdoor living space and your house is established before you begin, which simplifies the planning process. In most localities, you will need a building permit unless most of the structure you're enclosing is already in existence.

Construction is usually a matter of adding posts, beams, and a roof to the floor you already have; an outdoor area that's already covered makes the job that much easier. If you use your patio or deck as the base for a pre-manufactured screened-room kit, you can complete your project in a matter of days.

Before you enclose your patio or deck, you may need to modify it for your screened room. For example, you may need to pour new footings so that your patio or deck can support an overhead structure. Or you may need to skirt the base of a deck with screening to prevent bugs from entering through spaces between the decking boards (when building a new deck, screening can be placed over the supporting joists before decking is installed to solve this problem). Check with your local building department about any special requirements before you begin construction.

◀ **GARDEN ROOM**
Lush with greenery, this tile-floored patio brings the garden indoors.

▼ DINING DECK

Screened walls and skylights provide a generous serving of natural light in this outdoor dining space.

▲ PROTECTED BREEZEWAY

This screened patio incorporates elements that reflect the house's vintage style.

▶ EXPANSIVE SCREENED DECK

This large screened-in deck offers plenty of room—for lounging, dining, and more.

screened-room additions

A new screened room can lower electric bills, raise the curb appeal of your home, and increase its value. When adding on a new room, your options for function and style are wide open.

Adding a screened room to your house can expand your living space, bring light and air to the indoors, reduce your air-conditioning bill, and increase the value of your property—all for a price that's far lower than the cost of building a conventional room addition. As versatile as it is prac-tical, a screened addition can take any form you please, whether you want a modest space or a palatial one, an alfresco dining area or a spill-proof outdoor playroom.

Building a screened-room addi-tion from the ground up gives you all kinds of options that aren't available when you're enclosing a porch or patio. You can situate your new structure to catch the morning sun, cool the interior of your house, or capture your favorite view. Since you're creat-ing the footprint for your room, it can be any size that fits your needs and your yard. Choose your ceiling height. Create access to whatever interior room seems most convenient. Add columns or molding if you fancy them. Place the door wherever you like. Though you don't have a porch, deck, or patio to build upon,

▶ ***MAJOR ENHANCEMENT***
With a new screened addition, this small bungalow gained a whole new look.

▼ ***ELEGANT DETAILING***
This friendly screened entry is capped by solid roofing and translucent panels.

◀ **ARCHITECTURAL CONTINUITY**
Terra-cotta roofing on this screened-room addition visually ties it to the house's style.

▲ **LIVING ROOM**
The house's original exterior wall was preserved as an interesting focal point of this open-air living/dining room addition.

CORNER GAZEBO
The angled walls of this gazebo-like
room at one end of the house offer
classic charm and views.

◄ **PANORAMIC BACKDROP**
*From inside the room, guests can
enjoy an expansive view while rocking
on the classic porch swing.*

you're not constrained by pre-
existing design flaws or someone
else's taste.

When you're starting from
scratch, creating a screened room
is a major home improvement
project. You'll need to select and
prepare a site, keeping in mind
landscape features, sight lines,
traffic patterns, and microclimates. Your project will require
detailed drawings, and probably
a building permit. Design and
planning issues are significant:
Architectural styles must blend;
rooflines and siding must be tied
in with your house; materials
must match or complement the
main structure. You may need the
services of an engineer to ensure
that your structure is safe. The
construction process, which includes pouring a foundation and

building a roof, is best accomplished by a highly experienced
do-it-yourselfer.

Because there are so many factors to consider, you may want
professional help when you're
planning and constructing a
screened-room addition. You can
hire consultants to advise you, or
you can turn the entire project
over to a contractor. If you want
one-stop shopping and speedy
construction, you can sign on
with a company that specializes in
building pre-manufactured patio
rooms; in many cases you'll be
able to plan your screened room
in a couple of hours and installation will take only a few days. Ask
your builder or patio-room dealer
to add replaceable windows, and
you'll be able to use your screened
room almost all year long.

▲ **NEW FACADE**
*This elaborate screened entry
adds grace and ornate detail to
the house's exterior.*

garden rooms and pavilions

When set apart from the house, a screened room can take on its own charm, becoming a private retreat... or a busy center for activities.

A screened garden room or pavilion is a vacation destination in your own backyard. While an attached screened room brings the outdoors in, a freestanding structure draws you out of the house to the garden, cooling breezes, or splendid scenery.

When you set your screened room apart from your house, you open up a world of possibilities. You can position your garden room or pavilion to take maximum advantage of a view, or build it next to the pond so you can hear the water lapping. Put it where the outdoor action is, and it becomes a boathouse, a poolside cabana, or a place to unwind after a set of tennis. Take an indoor activity outdoors by creating a screened home office, breakfast nook, or reading area amid the flowers.

A screened garden room or pavilion offers a wide range of design choices. You can configure it to fit your needs rather than the dimensions of your house, and you won't have to worry about

▲ **COMFORTABLY CONNECTED**
Separate from the house but connected by a covered breezeway, this seaside sitting room offers breathtaking views.

tying in rooflines or siding. Choose any architectural style you like, as long as it harmonizes with the landscape and the surrounding buildings.

Building a stand-alone screened room presents many of the same challenges you'd encounter when constructing an addition to your home, though you will not have to deal with any existing structure or walls. You can keep your project manageable by choosing a site that's accessible and fairly level, an uncomplicated design that uses standard-size lumber, and ordinary materials that won't require professional installation services.

▲ BREEZY BOATHOUSE

An on-the-water retreat is a great draw for people—and bugs—making it a prime candidate for screening.

◄ POOLSIDE CABANA

Perched by a pool, this small pavilion offers a pest-free place for dining.

gazebos

Classic in style and functional in form, gazebos can be custom designed and built, or purchased as easy-to-assemble kits.

Gazebos are timeless symbols of gracious living. A gazebo's distinctive profile, intricate detailing, and elegant demeanor make it a classic structure. Screening will make it bug-free as well.

If your yard has a gorgeous garden or a breathtaking view, a screened gazebo offers an especially delightful way to take advantage of it. The word "gazebo" comes from the phrase "gaze about," and with its panoramic perspective, a gazebo definitely lives up to its name. Its octagonal shape also makes it an arresting focal point in your landscape.

Building an elaborate gazebo is well beyond the capabilities of the average handy homeowner. If you want to do the job yourself, you can use a simplified design that doesn't require you to cut compound angles and shape wood. Alternatively, you can purchase a gazebo kit that takes just a few days to assemble. Both options will require you to pour a concrete foundation that meets local code requirements. Many plans and kits feature a traditional open-air design, but adding screening is a relatively straight-forward task: You can staple screening directly to your structure, or construct removable screened frames to fit each opening (see page 40).

Gazebos typically measure from 10 to 16 feet across—a size that's modest enough for a small yard but large enough to seat four for dinner. A spacious screened pavilion may be more practical if you love to throw big parties, but for intimate gatherings and quiet contemplation, a screened gazebo can offer just what you need: maximum charm in a minimally sized package.

▲ **DESIRABLE DETAILS**
Though small in scale, this gazebo features removable window screens and an interesting floor configuration.

◀ POND-SIDE PAVILION

Nestled among pond lilies, this simple yet elegant structure boasts large screened bays and a cupola for ceiling ventilation.

◀ LAKESIDE RESORT

This breezy free-standing natural wood cabana matches the adjacent deck; inside, a hammock stretches from wall to wall above the intricate floor.

▼ FOREST'S EDGE

Accents on this poolside sitting room perfectly complement the matching latticework fence.

sleeping porches
and pool enclosures

*A screened specialty structure, such as a sleeping porch
or a pool enclosure, can dramatically improve your enjoyment
of the great outdoors.*

When the air is hot and the bugs are biting, you may yearn for a cool place to sleep, or a pest-free spot by the swimming pool. That's when you want a screened structure that serves a very specific purpose.

A screened sleeping porch is usually a simple structure, often just large enough to accommodate a bed. Popularized a century ago as a fresh-air remedy for a host of ailments, the sleeping porch now serves a more humble function, providing nighttime refuge from stifling heat and sterile air conditioning. It may appear wherever there's a sliver of extra space—above a covered patio or sunroom, adjacent to a bedroom, or even at the far end of the property. If your house has a small bal-cony or deck, you can turn it into a screened sleeping porch in the exact same way you would enclose a patio.

A screened pool covering provides a multitude of benefits. It not only keeps bugs from creating a nuisance, it prevents them from thrashing around in the water along with leaves, twigs, and other pool-clogging flotsam and jetsam that can make clean-up a Sisyphean ordeal. A screened enclosure will also block the sun's glare, and it can prevent accidents in one of your home's most potentially dangerous areas—a particularly important considera-

▲ **OUTDOOR BEDROOM**
*The contours of this airy sleeping
porch mirror the slope of the hill. Its
corrugated metal roof sheds rain while
the screening repels pests.*

tion if you have children or pets.

A pool enclosure is a monumental structure that will dominate the landscape, so take care to choose a style that complements that of your home and yard. Such a large-scale project can present construction challenges, as well: You'll need building permits, plenty of time, and probably a contractor to assist you. If you'd rather not tackle the job yourself, or if you'd like extras such as a retractable roof, consider hiring a company that specializes in pool-enclosure systems.

▶ **BASIC COVERAGE**

A single-level screened structure protects the pool and spa from insects and leaves.

screened rooms in new homes

Building a new home? Where flying insects can make outdoor living miserable, consider including a screened retreat in your plans.

The ideal time to think about creating a screened room, of course, is before your house is built. When you're planning a new home, you have a unique opportunity to design the ideal screened room to become an integral part of your dream house.

Screened rooms are prevalent in expensive new homes, and many architects routinely include them in new-home plans. No longer the narrow, enclosed architectural appendage of days past, today's screened room is a spacious, open, integral part of the whole house.

Starting with a blank slate gives you a wide array of possibilities for creating a bug-free outdoor area. You can wrap your screened room around the entire house, perch it above a precipice, or incorporate it into a second-story balcony. Position it to capture a fabulous view or a prevailing breeze. Choose any architectural style, from ultra-contemporary to classic Colonial. No matter what type of house you're planning, you can design a screened room to match.

Building your screened room along with your house also makes the construction process more efficient. There are no walls to knock down, no retrofits to wrestle with, no residents to disturb. Plumbing and/or electrical can be easily placed in open walls, and it's simpler to add luxuries such as a fireplace. Materials can be purchased for the house and for the screened structure at the same time, providing economies of scale and ensuring a seamless appearance.

If you want your new house to include a screened-in area, look for an architect who has experience creating screened environments. It should be planned and designed with careful forethought, and constructed with the same quality materials as the rest of your home.

SOUTHERN COMFORT
Stretching from corner to corner, this screened porch offers the perfect place to relax and enjoy the warm Florida evenings.

▲ **RANCH HOUSE**

This rugged, open-air screened porch, suited to the house's rural style, provides a protected hallway between rooms.

◄ **TREE LEVEL**

A voluminous wedge-shaped contemporary screened-in deck stands in stylized contrast to the surrounding landscape.

A screened room can be designed
for visual impact, as evidenced
by this stylish sitting room.

planning and design

A SCREENED ROOM HAS TO DO MORE THAN JUST KEEP OUT INSECTS.

It must suit your lifestyle, withstand the elements, and harmonize with your house, both inside and out. You may want it to provide privacy, sun control, or a view of the garden. And, of course, it should fit your price range and comply with all legal restrictions. Creating a structure that can do all that requires careful planning. ■ *This chapter provides an overview of the issues to consider before you begin building your screened room. You'll find information on site selection, materials, and design. You'll learn about the options for constructing a screened room, so you can decide whether to design and build one from scratch, assemble one from a kit, or hire a designer and/or contractor to*

build one. You'll also get tips on working with professionals and writing contracts. ■ *Whether you plan to do all, some, or none of the work yourself, this chapter will help you develop a game plan for your project. Your payback will be a screened room that's right for your family.*

evaluating your needs

The first step in planning your screened room is to pinpoint your priorities so you can tailor the structure to fit your family's preferences and needs.

Start the planning process by deciding what the primary function of your screened room will be. Do you want an alfresco dining room? A pool enclosure? A quiet spot where you can sit and read? If you want a peaceful sanctuary, a screened gazebo in a secluded corner of the garden may be just the thing; if outdoor dining is your top priority, perhaps you'd be better off with an attached screened room close to the kitchen.

Next, ask yourself a few other important questions.

HOW MUCH USE WILL YOUR SCREENED ROOM GET? Do you expect it to be a popular central gathering place? If so, it will need to be easily accessible from the house and spacious enough to accommodate your whole family. Will you venture into it only occasionally, when leisure time and comfortable temperatures coincide? Then a more modest structure will probably do. If you're unsure of how much time you'll spend in your screened room, err toward greater usage because you'll probably find that your family and guests prefer a bug-free outdoor space to an interior one that's oppressively hot or artificially cooled.

WHAT'S YOUR LIFESTYLE? A screened room won't get much use unless it suits the way your family lives. As you plan your structure, think about your lifestyle. Do you like to nap in a hammock on summer afternoons? If you do, it may be best to situate your screened room in the shade. On the other hand, if you're at the office all day, you may want your structure to catch the early morning sun or the evening breeze. Your lifestyle may affect your choice of materials, as well. For instance, you can opt for special heavy-duty screening if kids and pets are in the picture, or install an easy-upkeep concrete floor if you are a reluctant housekeeper (see Selecting Materials on page 30).

WHAT'S THE CLIMATE IN YOUR AREA? How much of the year you can enjoy your screened room will depend on your climate and the structure's design. In a mild southern climate, an unheated screened room will be habitable for most of the year; in northern areas, it will be strictly a summertime retreat. If you want to

This garden gazebo caters to the need for solitude, serving as a peaceful getaway far from the home's hustle and bustle.

stretch the screened-room "season," your plan can include extras such as solar screening, which will keep your structure from baking in the summer heat, or removable windows, which will keep it warm on cool days.

Scorching temperatures, high humidity, heavy snowfall, and other extreme weather conditions are planning issues, as well. You'll need to design and build your structure to survive any punishment your climate can dish out.

When it comes to choosing a

Above: Nestled in a lush garden area, this screened pavilion makes communing with nature perfectly bug-free. *Left:* An outdoor fireplace and pull-down shades make dining in this screened patio a multiseason possibility.

site for your screened structure, the microclimates of your lot are key. To be as comfortable as possible, your screened room should be properly oriented to the sun, shade, and wind patterns that are typical for your particular yard (see Selecting a Site on page 27).

DO YOU NEED PRIVACY? If you live in an area where houses are built closely together, you may want your screened room to provide privacy. All screened structures afford some seclusion, simply because they're enclosed. But you can plan your screened room to supply an extra measure of protection. Try to pick a location that's out of the sight lines of neighbors and passersby. Take advantage of landscaping features that can provide protective coverage. And consider using special solar screening, which appears almost opaque from the outside but offers good visibility from inside (see page 90 for more about screening).

WHAT AMENITIES WOULD YOU LIKE?
While your project is still in the planning stages, think about whether you want to outfit your

screened room with utility connections, skylights, or built-ins. You should incorporate these into your design from the beginning because they can be quite expensive to add once you have completed construction. To decide what amenities you will need, consider again how you'll use your screened room. Artificial lighting is essential for any nighttime activity, and you may want electrical outlets so you can plug in a laptop computer or a stereo. A ceiling fan can be a godsend on muggy days, especially since screening cuts down on air flow, and a heater can make chilly evenings cozier and extend your screened room's usefulness into spring and fall. If space is tight, you may want to install built-in seating to maximize square

A ceiling fan and fireplace, combined with sliding doors that close off the screened bays, allow this outdoor room to serve comfortably year-round.

footage, or built-in storage for easy access to cushions, cookout supplies, or children's toys.

HOW CAN YOU BEST MAXIMIZE YOUR INVESTMENT? Presumably you're building a screened room for your own use and pleasure, but keep in mind as you're planning your structure that it also has the potential to increase the resale value of your house (in fact, screened rooms are becoming de rigueur in newly constructed luxury homes). If this is an important consideration for you, be extra certain that your screened room is well designed and constructed with care. Resist the temptation to save money by scrimping on materials or doing work that's beyond your capabilities. You may find it worthwhile to enlist the services of an architect or designer (see page 36 for more about working with professionals).

HOW BIG SHOULD YOUR SCREENED ROOM BE? The right size for your screened room depends on how you intend to use it. You'll need at least 6 to 8 feet of depth for a seating area and 8 to 10 feet of length to accommodate a small table with four chairs. Keep in mind that these are minimum space requirements; many screened structures are 16 to 20 feet deep or larger. These bigger screened rooms, which often have sets of French doors leading into the house, visually open up adjacent rooms and add substantial living space. Begin with your wish list of elements and plot a practical size to accommodate your needs.

Once you've decided how big a space you want, make sure that the length and height of your screened room will be in scale with your home. If you're building an addition to your house, don't let it overwhelm other architectural features. Conversely, don't make it so small that it looks like an afterthought.

design basics

Because a screened room is often a major addition to the house and landscape, it should be attractive, practical, and compatible with its surroundings. During planning, pay special attention to how your new structure will look with your house and yard.

Whether or not it's attached to your house, a screened room should harmonize with your home's ambiance and architectural style. For example, no matter how much you may love Doric columns, a neoclassical screened porch is probably not your best option if you own a split-level ranch. To avoid architectural cacophony, identify the design motifs that define your home's character, and then incorporate them into your screened room. Pay attention to large forms such as rooflines, as well as to decorative details such as millwork. If possible, use materials for your screened room that match those of your house.

When you're standing in your screened room, you should be able to look out on a pleasant slice of scenery rather than at the garbage cans or your neighbor's garage. To ensure an unobstructed vista of the yard, build your structure with large openings and minimal framework. Keep the roof high enough so it doesn't block your view; the lowest beam should be no lower than 6 feet, 8 inches from the floor. If you're building a detached screened room, place it so it doesn't obscure desirable landscape features when you look into the yard

from the house. It should add interest to the landscape—not dominate it.

SELECTING A SITE

Your screened room's location will be critical to comfortable and successful use of the space. When choosing a site, it's important to consider a number of factors, including the climate, the orientation of the sun, the topography of the yard, access from the house, and more. You'll also need to take

into consideration any building or zoning restrictions (see Legal Restrictions on page 28). Following is a closer look at these important factors.

SUN AND CLIMATE Be aware that certain areas of your property may be particularly susceptible to searing temperatures, strong winds, snow accumulation, or other extreme weather conditions.

In some cases, you can juxtapose your screened room with an existing building to temper the climate in either the screened room or the house. To keep your screened room cooler, position it in the shadow of your house; if your house is too hot, consider

Set apart from the house, this home away from home is nestled between large trees in a sunny meadow, a site that lends a perfect balance of sun and shade.

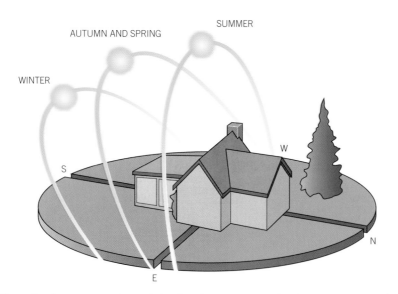

When planning a screened room's location, be sure to consider the room's orientation to the sun; note how the sun's arc changes from season to season.

building an attached screened room that will block the sun's glare and bring in fresh air.

When you're deciding what direction your screened room should face, pay particular attention to the path of the sun. A north-facing room will be coolest because the sun will rarely shine directly on it, and a south-facing room will be warmest because it will get sun all day. An eastern exposure will cause your screened room to heat up in the morning, and a western exposure will raise the temperature in the afternoon.

Which of these orientations is "best" depends on where you live. In Texas, a screened room that faces south could roast its occupants, but in Maine, it may get just the right amount of sunshine. Temperature regulation may not be your only priority. If you dream of watching the sunrise every morning, you may want an east-facing screened room even though a north-facing one would be cooler.

TOPOGRAPHY Although you can build on a site that's uneven, sloped, or otherwise challenging, it's best to situate your screened room on a flat, level surface. If you do opt for a difficult site, you may need help (see Choosing Professionals on page 35). As you're considering different locations, avoid areas with drop-offs, unstable soil, or poor drainage.

ACCESSIBILITY The site you select should be easily accessible from interior areas where people tend to gather; don't try to make use of "leftover" space in your yard unless you're prepared for your screened room to fall into disuse. You'll also need to make sure that the location you choose won't interfere with existing traffic patterns or block a view that you want to preserve.

MAKING A SITE WORK Of course, you may have no choice regarding where to put your screened room.

If you're enclosing an existing porch or swimming pool or there's only one spot in your yard that's level enough for building, your site is predetermined. In that case, your job is to make the best of the conditions you've been given. If your site is too sunny, you can use special solar screening to keep your screened room cooler. If a screened porch will make the house too dark, you can include skylights (space them evenly across the roof, and face them to the north, if you can, so the room won't become an oven). If you're forced to build within viewing distance of the neighbors, add shades for privacy. If you can't orient your room to catch prevailing breezes, stir up your own with a ceiling fan.

LEGAL RESTRICTIONS

Your local building department will probably have safety and zoning regulations that apply to residential additions and outdoor structures. Local ordinances may require you to obtain a permit to build your screened room.

In most areas, you won't need a permit to convert your deck, porch, or patio into a screened room, provided that the existing structure is on an approved lot plan. Screened rooms that can easily be disassembled and moved are also exempt from most local restrictions because they are considered temporary. However, chances are good that you'll need a permit to construct a permanent structure that's bigger than 10 feet square. Projects that include electrical wiring or plumbing may require permits for each process.

Permanent structures are usually subject to height limitations, setback requirements, and lot-coverage restrictions. Setback ordinances specify how close to the property line you may build, and lot-coverage restrictions determine how much of your property you're allowed to cover (an important consideration if you anticipate adding to your home in the future). Contact your local building department to find out what regulations apply in your area.

DRAWING A BASE MAP

For planning purposes, it's a good idea to make a scale drawing of your yard. A base map will be a helpful tool for designing a project or working with professionals, and it may be required by the building or planning department. In addition, it will allow you to visualize how your structure will fit in with its surroundings.

Make note of property setbacks, views you want to preserve, places that lack privacy, or any other areas of consideration. Careful attention to detail at this stage of the process will help you avoid unpleasant surprises.

To begin making a base map of your property, measure your yard, your house, and the distance from your house to the property line on all sides. Plot these distances on a sheet of drafting paper or graph paper, using any scale that's workable for you.

Be sure that your map includes the following:

- Dimensions of your lot
- Points of the compass showing how your house is situated on the lot
- Locations of rooms, doors, and windows in your house that will relate to the structure
- Size and location of any other structures, such as a pool, patio, or deck
- Location of utility lines near the new structure's location
- Setback lines
- Trees and other prominent landscape features
- Path and direction of the sun (note any "hot spots")
- Direction of prevailing winds
- Obstructions beyond the lot that may affect sun, wind, views, or privacy

When your map is complete, place a sheet of tracing paper over it, and then sketch out the footprint of your ideal screened room. You can then move the tracing paper around to see how your structure will fit in different locations. Once you have a design that pleases you, calculate what its actual dimensions would be, and then go outside and confirm its size and placement in your yard with a metal tape measure.

After you have planned your structure's dimensions and location, you can choose a project from this book's pages or work with a professional (see page 35) to flesh out a custom design.

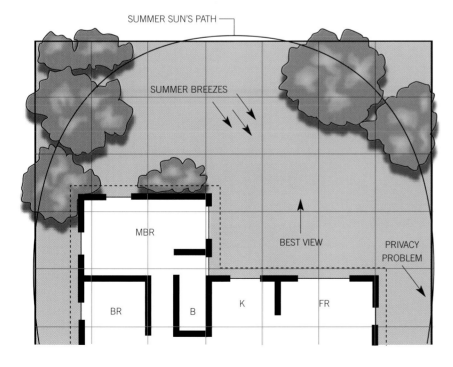

Before siting your screened room, make a scale drawing of your house and property, noting any special considerations.

selecting materials

Many different materials are used to build screened rooms. In choosing materials, you'll face numerous decisions and trade-offs that will dramatically affect the room's appearance, style, function, cost, and ease of construction.

Following is a general overview of key materials. For more specific material-buying information, see page 88.

STRUCTURAL COMPONENTS Most outdoor structures are made from wood, which is attractive, versatile, practical, and easily workable. A wooden screened room can be designed to blend with just about any house style, and it has a warm, authentic look that reflects the natural landscape. Wood products come in a wide variety of sizes, shapes, textures, and grades. Choose lumber for your structure's various components based on strength and durability requirements as well as visibility; make sure it has a straight grain so it won't warp and twist in changing weather conditions. (For more about choosing lumber, see pages 88–90).

To minimize the environmental impact of your purchase, you can seek out sustainably harvested "certified" wood. You can also use recycled or salvaged wood, which will hold its shape because it has already been weathered; it has a unique look that new wood simply can't match.

In some cases, you can substitute low-maintenance manufactured products for wood in your screened-room construction. Composite lumber (see page 89) is immune to water damage, decay, and pests, and it can be painted or stained.

ALUMINUM AND VINYL SYSTEMS
An aluminum or vinyl screened room offers affordability, rapid assembly, and low maintenance; the most popular screened-room kits come with vinyl or aluminum framing. Structures made from these materials often require professional installation, and they may leak if they're not well made. Aluminum and vinyl have a markedly different appearance

Above: Polyester screen-like fabric drapes gracefully from the cupola of this "brush arbor" gazebo. The bent tubular-steel construction is painted to resemble tree branches. *Left:* An aluminum screening system mimics the rooflines of this home and provides a house-wide insect shield, protecting everything from the upstairs deck to the garden.

than wood, of course, so choose them with care, particularly if you have an older house.

INTERIOR FINISHES For the inside of your screened room, select finish materials that are rugged enough for casual indoor/outdoor living. Durable exterior paints and stains will withstand dampness, extreme temperatures, snowfalls, and rainstorms; 100 percent acrylic formulations are generally preferred. Concrete, stone, or tile flooring will stand up to sudden thunderstorms and mud-covered kids on trikes. Acrylic fabrics for curtains or upholstery will resist soil and mildew.

Link your screened room to the interior of your house by using the same or complementary materials in both spaces. Natural materials such as wood and slate will help to create a pleasing flow from your structure to your yard.

SCREENING Choose your screening based on what you want it to do and how you want it to look. Any type of screening will provide an effective bug barrier, but you may also want your screens to regulate sunlight, provide privacy, match your copper gutters, or resist shredding by persistent pets.

Screening comes in a variety of materials. The two most common are aluminum and vinyl-coated fiberglass. If you're satisfied simply to keep mosquitoes at bay, one of these should suffice. Both are available in shades of black and

Finished wood decking, heavy mesh screens, and translucent ceiling panels are durable, attractive elements that seamlessly blend this dramatic perch with its surroundings.

gray, and aluminum screening is available with a clear coating that helps maintain its bright silver finish (though darker colors will provide better visibility from inside a screened room).

All screening blocks some sunlight, but for serious glare protection you'll need solar screening, made from tightly woven vinyl-covered fiberglass. Stamped aluminum and bronze screens that are capable of blocking out as much as 85 percent of sunlight are also available—but are very

expensive. Pet-resistant screening is made of vinyl-coated polyester that's heavier and seven times stronger than normal screening, so it resists shredding.

Before making any selection, unroll several feet of fabric and look through an unfurled section from a distance; it will look lighter from a few feet away. Also inquire about the screening's density, because it is not only the fiber of the material but also its thickness that determines its properties. (For more about screening, see page 90.)

creating a budget

Building a screened room can be an inexpensive proposition or a costly one, depending on how ambitious your project is and how much of the work you can do yourself.

To determine how much your structure will cost, start by calculating what you'll pay for your two biggest budget items: labor and materials.

If you're hiring a professional, get a bid or an estimate that will specify how much you'll pay for labor (see Working With Pros on page 36). Be sure that you've accounted for all the professional services you may require—for example, you may need an engineer to inspect your drawings. If you're doing the work yourself, remember that you may end up spending money to rent tools or rectify mistakes, so you should build such expenses into your budget. Also, don't simply assume that your labor is "free"; your time is worth money, and ultimately you may be better off hiring someone who can do the job faster and more efficiently, particularly if you will be forgoing income to work on your project.

To calculate the cost of materials, call several local merchants to compare prices (the chart on page 89 will help you determine what types and sizes of lumber you'll need to build a screened room from wood). Don't try to cut costs by using low-quality materials that won't survive repeated battering by the elements. Instead, consider downsizing your structure, or substitute durable but less expensive products for costly ones (a concrete floor instead of a slate one, for example). If you're buying a screened-room kit, you can save money by choosing vinyl or aluminum frames rather than wood, but beware of cheap products that are unattractive or poorly made.

If your budget is tight, you can incorporate money-saving measures right into your design plan. Your screened room will be most affordable if you can enclose an existing structure such as a patio or porch; if you're starting from scratch, consider building atop a ground-hugging wood deck instead of a concrete foundation. Rather than constructing custom-built screened frames to enclose your structure, try using ready-made screen-door panels instead. To keep down the cost of a screened-room kit, look for a design that has a rectangular shape and straight eaves.

Who says a screened addition has to be expensive? This kit-built room offers service and style at a reasonable price.

Many screened-room kits still require a relatively high level of building skills. Make sure you measure your time, talents, and tools before tackling such a project.

getting it built

Building your own screened room can save you money and give you total control over the project. The key is to select a project that matches your abilities.

Many of the screened rooms in this book can be tackled by a do-it-yourselfer with a reasonable amount of experience, but keep in mind that any given project will be more difficult if you're dealing with a variable such as a challenging location or poor soil conditions.

Be honest with yourself about how much time you can devote to your role as a part-time screened-room builder, and don't give yourself an unreasonable deadline; plan to spend at least 150 hours building your structure, and allow extra time for mistakes. Before you begin your project, plot out a construction schedule and arrange for materials to be delivered in the proper sequence. Make sure that you have all the tools you'll need and any permits your local building department requires. Remember that there may be indirect costs involved in doing your own construction; you probably won't save much money if you have to rent equipment or take time off from your job to complete the project.

Hire professionals to work on your project if you're inexperienced, over-scheduled, or simply unwilling to spend the better part of several weekends building a screened room. An expert can be indispensable if you're dealing with electrical and plumbing work, building permits and inspectors, a difficult site, or hard-to-handle materials. You can let a general contractor oversee the entire construction process, or you can hire subcontractors with specific skills to do some or all of the work. If you act as your own general contractor, you'll be the one supervising subcontractors, ordering materials, keeping records, and obtaining permits. Even if your project poses no unusual challenges, you may want to hand it over to a professional simply to speed up the construction process and buy yourself some free time. (For tips on working with pros, see page 36.)

ASSEMBLING A KIT

Building your screened room from a kit can be faster and easier than starting from scratch, and there are options to fit every budget and skill level.

The simplest and least expensive type of kit forms a collapsible free-standing structure that can be put together in less than an hour and quickly disassembled for winter storage. These relatively low-cost kits, which run from about $700 to $1,300, are available in sizes ranging from about 90 to 220 square feet, in both round and rectangular configurations. They are best located over a patio or deck, but some can be set up right in your yard, though the latter will require site preparation.

A kit for building a permanent screened room can be anything from a simple frame with screened panels to a sunroom-type structure with windows that slide away or pop out to make way for screens in the summertime. A few companies offer kits made of wood, but vinyl and aluminum are more common and much less expensive. Though some kits require considerable building skills, many are made to bolt together quite easily, with color-coded components and hardware included. For ease of installation, pick a modular system with straight eaves. But even for the simplest of kits, plan on having a helper assist you.

For even simpler setup, you can buy a pre-assembled screened room that will be delivered to your home and ready to use in a matter of hours. If you intend to use your screened room in cooler weather, look for a "three-season" model with an insulated roof (laminated aluminum panels with a 3-inch foam core will be adequate for most climates).

If you have an existing room you'd like to convert to a screened room, you can simply replace one wall with a folding window-wall system. The window "wall" is actually a series of screened panels that open like an accordion. The panels glide smoothly on ball bearings and lock securely when closed. Although pricey, window-wall systems have a unique, open look. They are relatively easy to install and can be manufactured to standard or custom sizes.

You can buy a screened-room kit from a local patio-room company or one of several major manufacturers (see Screened-Room Builders on page 37). Be aware that some manufacturers sell only through contractors who will charge a fee to assemble your

Cost-effective and relatively quick to construct, kit-built screened rooms such as this provide myriad design options that can be tailored to fit almost any home.

structure for you. If you want to lower your costs, ask if you can help with the construction. In any case, remember that you will be responsible for obtaining any building permits.

Keep in mind that the majority of problems (such as leakage) that plague screened rooms are caused by improper installation. Be sure to follow instructions exactly and get professional help if you need it. Manufacturers' warranties cover only defective merchandise; if a product malfunctions because of incorrect installation, the responsibility is yours.

CHOOSING PROFESSIONALS

Chances are that you'll want at least some professional assistance as you're designing and building your screened room. You can turn the entire job over to a general contractor, or hire a specialist to help you with a particular phase of the process. Depending on the help you need, you can call on the following professionals:

ARCHITECTS AND LANDSCAPE ARCHITECTS Licensed by the state and trained to create structurally sound, aesthetically satisfying designs, they can select and procure materials and supervise all phases of construction.

LANDSCAPE AND BUILDING DESIGNERS These usually unlicensed professionals are trained in landscape architecture; some of them also offer construction services.

Perfecting the sweeping curves of this seaside home's screened walls is the type of work best left to a seasoned professional.

DRAFTSPERSONS A draftsperson can create the drawings you'll need in order to secure a building permit; you or your contractor can work from these drawings when constructing your screened room. If you're modifying a plan in this book, a qualified draftsperson may be all you need.

ENGINEERS These professionals can ensure that your structure will withstand any stress caused by strong winds, heavy loads, or unstable soil. A soils engineer will establish design specifications for your structure's foundation if you're building on a steep or unstable lot. A structural engineer can provide wind- and load-stress calculations and make certain your structure has the strength to perform its function safely.

GENERAL AND LANDSCAPE CONTRACTORS Specialists in construction or landscape construction, they may do all or some of the work themselves or supervise subcontractors. Most will obtain permits for you, and some have design experience, as well.

SUBCONTRACTORS These are contractors who specialize in a certain aspect of construction, such as carpentry, masonry, grading, electrical, or plumbing. If you act as your own general contractor, it will be your responsibility to hire, coordinate, and supervise subcontractors and obtain permits. Subcontractors will perform the work according to your drawings. Some will also provide product information and procure materials for the project.

The steeply pitched roof and intricate wood detailing of this Cape Cod pavilion are the sorts of custom details that require professional design help.

WORKING WITH PROS

Once you've determined the kind of person or persons you want to hire, you have several options for establishing a working relationship. If you'd like someone to offer suggestions or review your plans, you can pay a professional an hourly or daily rate to act as a consultant (subcontractors may also charge by the hour, particularly if the job is small). For a specific job that can be clearly defined—for example, you want someone to create working drawings or pour a foundation—you can negotiate a flat fee. If you want a professional to handle your project from start to finish, you can get a contractor or designer to bid on everything from planning through construction.

To find a qualified professional in your area, get recommendations from friends and neighbors.

Interview several candidates who have experience working on projects like yours, and check their credentials (an architect should have a state license and an architecture degree, and a general or landscape contractor should be licensed and bonded). If you're hiring someone on a planning-through-construction basis, request a written, itemized bid that includes a breakdown of time, materials costs, and labor rates. If you'll be paying an hourly rate, ask how long the job will take, and find out whether you can obtain a "not to exceed" figure. Before you sign a contract, ask to see some finished work. Most design and construction professionals can supply photographs of the projects they've completed, and some will even arrange for you to visit former clients' homes.

WRITING A CONTRACT

Even when you're confident you've found trustworthy, skilled professionals, it's important to have a written contract in order to avoid misunderstandings and help settle any disputes.

Some items to include are:
- Start and finish dates.
- The right to settle disputes by arbitration, which can often be speedier and less costly than a court proceeding.
- A warranty of at least a year on all work and materials. Some states require a warranty of five years on all work and ten years for hidden problems.
- A payment schedule. Never pay more than 10 percent or $1,000, whichever is lower, upfront. The final payment should be made only upon satisfactory completion of the job.
- Detailed job and materials descriptions. If you want a stamped-concrete floor in a certain color, put it in writing.
- A waiver of subcontractor liens. In some states, subcontractors can place a lien on your property if the general contractor fails to pay them. To protect yourself from this consequence, specify that you will not make the final payment until the contractor gives you an unconditional release of these rights from all subcontractors and suppliers who provided services or materials.
- If amendments, or "change orders," are made along the way, be sure both parties initial them.

SCREENED-ROOM BUILDERS

If you're looking for one-stop shopping, you can hand your entire project over to a company that specializes in building pre-manufactured patio rooms. Though this is not your cheapest option, it usually costs less than hiring an assortment of professionals to design and create a one-of-a-kind structure from scratch. It is also by far the simplest way to go, often requiring little more than an in-home consultation and, perhaps, a showroom visit.

The company you hire will deal with all engineering issues, local permits, and building codes. (Ask to see the state's engineering stamp on the design.) The construction process takes only a few days, and components and installation are typically covered by warranty.

Pre-manufactured patio rooms are factory-built products that can be ordered off the shelf or customized to fit almost any situation. The majority are aluminum and vinyl structures that sell for an average of $20,000, but some are luxurious edifices of wood and thermal glass that can cost $100,000 or more, depending on site issues and other factors.

Most manufacturers offer two options: a "three-season" room with single-pane windows or a heated, fully insulated "four-season" room suitable for year-round use. Both types are basically sunrooms that can be converted to screened rooms in warm weather. Depending on where you live and how persistent you are, you can also find companies that will sell you a room with screened panels and no windows, known in the industry as a "two-season" room. To get an idea of what you can expect from each type of structure, check with the National Sunroom Association (see Resources on page 128), which has developed standards for the various categories.

Many areas have local and regional builders who advertise themselves as patio-room specialists. These smaller companies

This pre-manufactured patio room features the charming lines of a multifaceted English conservatory.

can offer flexibility and personal attention (for example, they may build you a two-season room even if it's not one of their standard offerings), and some have expertise in a particular area, such as high-end construction. If you decide you want to hire a local patio-room company, be sure to ask for references and choose one that's been operating successfully for a number of years. Growing competition and complicated building codes are making it increasingly difficult for small outfits to stay afloat; though many offer excellent products and service, some will go out of business before your warranty expires.

The major patio-room manufacturers offer reliability and continuity of service. Most depend on dealers or franchises to install their products (one notable exception is the industry's No. 1 manufacturer, Champion Window Mfg. Co., which installs and services every patio room it sells). As a rule, local dealers are quite competent; many are well-established contractors who have decided to get into the patio-room business. If a franchise folds, the parent company will generally obligate another local franchise to honor your warranty.

In some parts of the country, you may find it difficult to purchase a fully installed patio room from one of the major manufacturers. Only the oldest of the top three companies, Four Seasons Sunrooms, sells and installs its products in all 50 states. Champion operates in 28 states and will not sell its products in other areas. Patio Enclosures Inc., which has distributors on the East Coast and in the Midwest, will sell you a do-it-yourself patio-room kit if you don't live near a distributor who can install a structure for you. Four Seasons franchises can also sell you one of the company's patio rooms so you can assemble it yourself (or hire your own contractor to do it), but the company cautions that some of its installations are beyond the skill level of an amateur builder.

A unique rope-and-pulley system for raising and lowering the window sashes instantly turns this screened room into a three-season room (see page 76).

screened-room projects

IN THIS CHAPTER, YOU WILL FIND A VARIETY OF DO-IT-yourself projects, including plans and step-by-step building instructions for them. They range from simple weekend jobs, such as hanging a screen door, to far more complex undertakings that require a much higher skill level, such as adding on a screened room. Even if you consider yourself a seasoned do-it-yourselfer, consult a professional if the challenges seem a bit beyond your skill level. ■ *The intent of this chapter is to present a range of basic projects that will work in a variety of situations. Though the plans may not correspond exactly to your circumstance, they can serve as a starting point. You can tailor a project to suit your needs, as long as you build the structure according to standard structural practices. When in doubt, hire an architect or designer to assist you. Be sure to ask your local building department about the need for plan checking or permits.*

attaching screening

Does your home have a covered porch? If it does, imagine how much more enjoyable it would be if it were screened to keep the bugs out. Screening-in a porch is a relatively easy job, as you'll discover here.

You can use any of several methods to screen-in a porch. The best one will depend on your situation and whether or not you want the screening to be removable. Some porches have framed-in bays, others have just a post or column at each corner. If the bays are framed-in with window-like openings, the job will be easy. If the porch has only a couple of columns or posts, you'll need to build a framework to hold the screening. The instructions on these pages assume that your porch has a roof that fully extends over the porch floor and that it needs such a framework; omit or modify any of the steps that don't apply to your situation.

Stretching and stapling screening across framed openings is generally fast, easy, and inexpensive, but permanent, which may not be desirable. And, with this method, screening is prone to sag or bag. To screen an opening this way, make sure to keep the screen mesh at right angles to the frame. Staple across the top, and then the bottom, and then along the sides of the frame. Stretch the screening as taut as possible, stapling every 2 inches, as you work from the center outward. Cover the stapled edges with 3/8-by-3/4-inch battens and secure them with 3d galvanized nails.

An alternative method, installing removable screens, is a bit more involved because it calls for careful measuring and for having framed screens made or making them yourself. But, in the long run, removable screens are far more convenient because you can take them off for repair or when you do not need or want them. It's also much easier to stretch screening tight across removable

A gridwork of permanently screened bays protects this airy nook yet offers an easy, open connection with the yard.

frames. For more about this, see the instructions on page 43.

Although you can make framed screens yourself, having them made by a professional screen shop is usually a very affordable, reliable option. For information about screening fabrics, see page 90. Yet another easy, relatively inexpensive choice is to use a vinyl-spline system to mount the screening (see below).

Above left: Large screen frames were designed to span the distance between support posts on this porch. *Above right:* Screen frames were custom fit to these unusually shaped bays, which have angled top corners. Twist clips hold the frames in place.

VINYL-SPLINE SYSTEM

For screening that's particularly easy to install and replace, check out vinyl-spline screen-attachment systems (sold under the trade name Screen Tight™). These systems use base-attachment tracks and vinyl splines to lock screening into place. The vinyl components, which can be cut with pruning shears, allow for quick, professional-looking installation at a relatively low cost. To install:

1. Use 1-inch screws to attach the system's vinyl channels along each edge of the frame. Drive the screws through the screw slots along the entire length of each mounting strip.

2. Stretch screening over each opening, making sure the mesh is at right angles to the frame.

3. Tape the screening in place, beginning at the top and working your way down the sides.

4. Feed the top-edge spline into the track and, using the concave end of a screening tool, roll it securely into place.

5. Remove the tape, and roll-in the bottom edge. Follow with the sides and mid-rail, if the screen has one. Make sure you keep the screening as taut as possible during this process.

6. Use a utility knife to trim off the excess screening, and snap trim caps onto the splines. If a trim cap is too long, cut it to size with pruning shears.

7. Make sure each butt joint aligns with the joints of the frame. Gently hammer the trim caps over the channels with a mallet to lock the screens in place.

Top: Parts of the spline system's base channel are easily cut to fit, using pruning shears, and then butted together and screwed to the frame. *Above:* Once screening is fastened onto channels, the cap piece is tapped into place and trimmed with the shears.

HOW TO BUILD A FRAMEWORK FOR SCREENS

1 **Cut a 2-by-4 top plate** to fit between the porch posts. Hold it in position along the ceiling, and nail it to firm backing with 16d galvanized nails. If you can't nail it to a beam, secure it to joists with two 16d nails per joist. If the top plate runs parallel to the joists, install nailing blocks between the joists and fasten the plate to them. Then drop a plumb bob from the top plate so you can position the bottom plate directly beneath it. Measure the distance between posts on the floor, and cut the 2-by-4 bottom plate. Position the bottom plate on the floor, and cut away the section where the screen door will go. If the floor is wood, attach the pieces with 16d galvanized nails, staggered and spaced every 16 inches. If the floor is concrete, use masonry anchors (see page 92).

2 **Use stud-framing clips** to install wall studs or posts where needed. (Where clips would be visible, toenail each stud or post to the top and bottom plates with 12d nails.) Studs that will support siding or wall coverings are typically placed on 16- or 24-inch centers. Cut the supports to length, and then lift them into position, flush with the edges of the top and bottom plates. Check plumb, and secure them to the plates.

3 **Cut 2-by-4 knee rails** to fit between the posts and studs, and cut 2-by-4 supports for each end of each knee rail. Toenail the knee-rail supports to the bottom plate, and nail them to the posts and/or studs. Then toenail the knee rails to the posts and studs.

4 **Assemble screen** surrounds from beveled 1 by 4s to fit in the openings formed by the support members. Nail 1-by-1 stops flush with the outside edges of the frames. Nail the screen surrounds into place in the openings. Check the corners for square as you work, and adjust the surrounds, if necessary. Secure the screen frames to the 1-by-1 stops with 1½-inch galvanized screws, driven at an angle. To remove the screens for repair or storage, simply remove the screws.

STEP 1

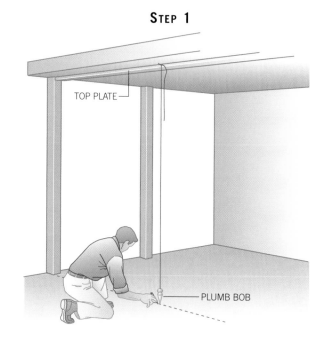

TOP PLATE

PLUMB BOB

STEP 2

STUD-FRAMING CLIP

LEVEL

POST (OR STUD)

STEP 3

STEP 4

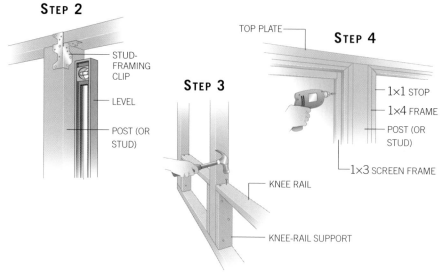

TOP PLATE

1×1 STOP

1×4 FRAME

POST (OR STUD)

1×3 SCREEN FRAME

KNEE RAIL

KNEE-RAIL SUPPORT

MAKING FRAMED SCREENS

1 **Measure the openings,** and then assemble 1 by 3s as screen frames to fit. Unless you're experienced at making dowel or biscuit joints, butt-join the frames at the corners and fasten the pieces with ¾-inch galvanized screws and flat L-shaped metal brackets. (Attach the brackets to both sides.)

2 **Lay a frame** on a piece of plywood, and slide ½-inch-thick wood strips under the top and bottom of the frame. Slightly bow the center by tightening C-clamps or woodworker's clamps around the frame and the plywood at the midpoint of the two sides.

For a small screen, you can use a cleat and wedges to draw the screening fabric tight. Staple the screening along the top edge of the frame, stretch it to the opposite edge, and temporarily attach a cleat to the plywood. Insert wedges between the cleat and the frame on both sides, and gently tap them together until the screening is tight.

3 **Cut a piece of screening** slightly wider and longer than the frame, and lay the fabric across the frame. (You may have to temporarily remove the clamps during this stage.) Adjust the mesh so it's at right angles to the frame, and then staple it across the center of the frame's top edge with rust-proof staples spaced every 2 inches, working from the middle

outward. Repeat along the bottom edge. Release the clamps to straighten out the frame, which will pull the screening taut. Then

staple the screening to the sides, working from the middle outward as you did before. Trim off the excess screening.

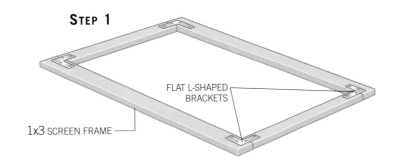

STEP 1

FLAT L-SHAPED BRACKETS

1x3 SCREEN FRAME

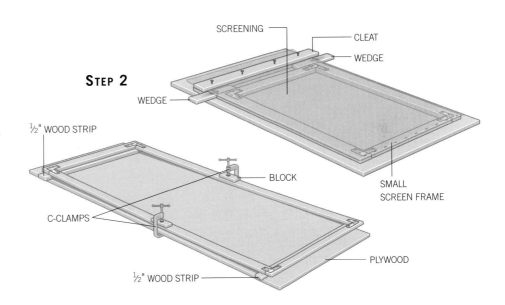

STEP 2

SCREENING

CLEAT

WEDGE

WEDGE

½" WOOD STRIP

BLOCK

SMALL SCREEN FRAME

C-CLAMPS

PLYWOOD

½" WOOD STRIP

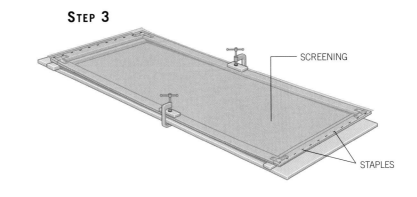

STEP 3

SCREENING

STAPLES

enclosing a patio

In this simplest of attached screened rooms, the structural members support only a lightweight roof and the screens.

Built over an existing brick, tile, flagstone, or concrete patio, this structure requires little in the way of materials and is easy and inexpensive to construct. But the payoff is wonderful: a big, bright, bug-free space to take in the evening breezes and garden view.

Of course, other options for this type of screened space include more substantial structures, such as those shown on pages 8–9 (see also the projects on pages 48 and 54), but this one is a perfect example of the "less is more" philosophy.

DESIGN DETAILS

The three-sided structure consists of a series of modular bays and so is vertically scalable. We've used 4-foot-wide modules for the sides and 3 footers for the front, yielding a 15-by-12-foot room. You can vary the dimensions of the bays slightly to fit your situation; just be sure each rafter end falls directly over an upright. To eliminate flashing problems, this structure is butted against the house underneath the roof overhang. Ceiling height drops from 10 feet in the rear to 9 feet in front.

All lumber is 2 by 4, with the exception of the 2-by-6 ledger, rafters, and blocking and the 4-by-4 corner posts. The translucent roof is made from fiberglass panels, but any similar lightweight material will do. The screens are simply stapled to the structural members, and then the edges are covered with lath. The screen door is a manufactured unit widely available at home improvement centers.

BUILDING NOTES

Plan for your project's footprint to fall at least 4 inches inside your patio perimeter. Even though the

The straightforward design of this screened patio makes it a project that can be accomplished in a couple of weekends. Materials are lightweight and inexpensive; butting the structure under the house's eaves eliminates the need for flashing. Leaving the wood natural instead of painting it reduces the labor even more.

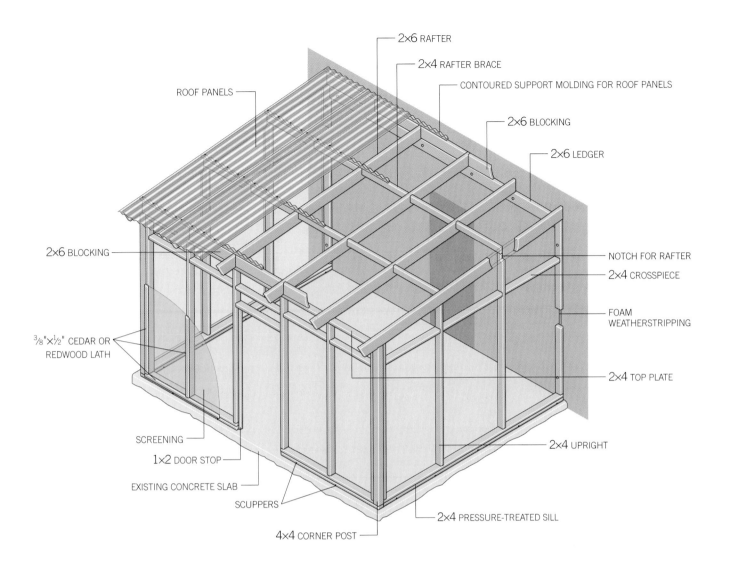

2×6 RAFTER

2×4 RAFTER BRACE

CONTOURED SUPPORT MOLDING FOR ROOF PANELS

2×6 BLOCKING

2×6 LEDGER

ROOF PANELS

NOTCH FOR RAFTER

2×4 CROSSPIECE

FOAM WEATHERSTRIPPING

2×6 BLOCKING

3/8"×1/2" CEDAR OR REDWOOD LATH

2×4 TOP PLATE

2×4 UPRIGHT

SCREENING

1×2 DOOR STOP

EXISTING CONCRETE SLAB

SCUPPERS

2×4 PRESSURE-TREATED SILL

4×4 CORNER POST

structure and roofing will be lightweight, the slab should be at least 6 inches thick, as discussed on page 99. Patios are already pitched for drainage—usually ¼ inch per foot—so you'll need to take this into account when cutting the members. If you plan to paint or stain the structure, do so after the frames are built and the rafters are cut but before they are assembled. As with any construction, check with your building department first to make sure the structure adheres to code. Buy the screen door before you build, and size the opening to fit it.

STEP-BY-STEP GUIDE

1 Lay out the 2-by-4 pressure-treated sills on the patio surface, checking diagonal measurements for square, as discussed on page 98. Mark and bore holes in the patio for masonry anchors and in the sills for galvanized lag screws, starting about 6 inches from the ends of each sill and then continuing every 4 feet. With a circular saw, cut ¾-inch-square "scuppers" (grooves) every 3 feet or so in the bottom edges of the sills to allow for drainage. Insert the anchors into the patio surface. Attach the

pressure-treated sills to the patio surface by driving the lag screws into the anchors. Create lap joints at the outer corners.

2 Erect and plumb the corner posts atop the sills. Support the posts with temporary diagonal braces running from the posts to the sills (1-by-4 lumber is good for this), and toenail the posts at the bottom. Temporarily fasten the braces with outdoor screws.

3 Build the wall frames (see page 125) flat on the patio, double checking measurements to ensure they will fit between the plumbed posts. Working from the 2-by-4 sill up, drill pilot holes for outdoor screws, and then fasten all joints with the screws. (Alternatively, you can use metal framing hardware to make the connections, trading appearance for added strength.) Finish the end frame with a 2-by-4 top plate.

4 **Erect the end frame**, fastening it temporarily to the corner posts with outdoor screws. Shim the frame atop the sill, if necessary, to level it. Follow with the side frames. Because of the patio's pitch, you may need to "rack" (force by pushing) the frames plumb. Fasten them permanently

with lag screws and washers, counterboring the 2 by 4s to accept the washers and driving the screws through the frames and into the 4-by-4 posts. Insert foam weatherstripping between the house and the side frames, and then fasten the frames to the house with anchors. Fasten the rear crosspieces to the uprights of the side frames and to the house. If you have painted the members, touch them up as needed.

5 **Install a ledger** as discussed on page 96. Rest a 2-by-6 rafter on the top plate of the end frame and on the ledger. Mark the rafter for the bird's-mouth cuts that will allow it to rest on the plate and

ledger, and then make the cuts. Use this rafter as a template to mark the other rafters (see page 116). Sight down all rafters to make sure the crowns point up, and then cut the boards. Finally, place a pair of rafters in position against the side uprights. Mark the rafters for 2-inch-deep notches, and then mark the side supports. Make the notch cuts, and cut the side supports to length.

6 **Paint or stain** the rafters, and then fasten them by driving outdoor screws at an angle into their supports. Now cut, paint or stain, and fasten 2-by-4 rafter braces between the rafters with outdoor screws. Add 2-by-6 blocking, ripped to the correct depth and angle, between the rafters where they rest on the top plate and ledger. Screw support molding to the top of the blocking and the top of the rafter braces. Fasten the roof panels according to the manufacturer's instructions.

7 **Staple screening** to the bays, working from top to bottom to stretch the material taut. (For more about attaching screening, see page 40.) Cover the edges by nailing prepainted lath or 1-by lumber to the supports. Finally, hang the screen door according to the manufacturer's directions.

SIDE ELEVATION VIEW

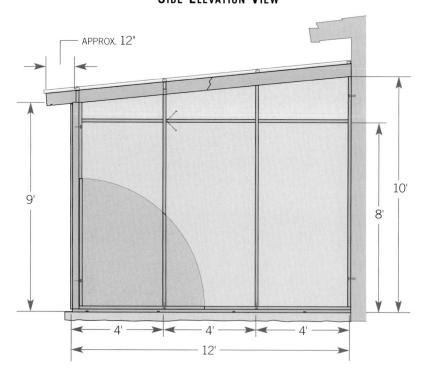

APPROX. 12"

9'

10'

8'

4'   4'   4'

12'

TOP PLAN VIEW

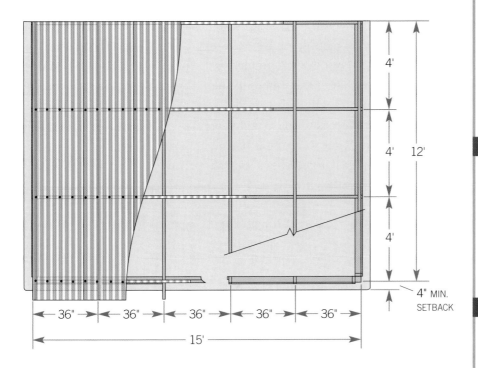

4'

4'

4'

12'

4" MIN.
SETBACK

36"   36"   36"   36"   36"

15'

FRONT ELEVATION VIEW

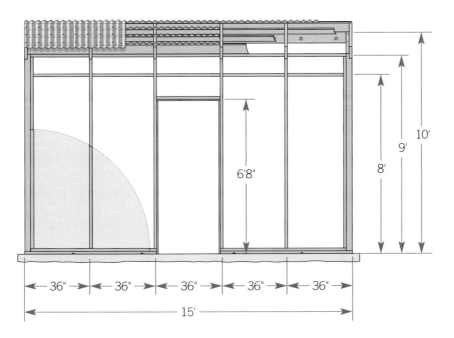

6'8"

10'

9'

8'

36"   36"   36"   36"   36"

15'

MATERIALS CHECKLIST

LUMBER

2x4 pressure-treated sills

2x4 framing

2x6 roof framing

2x6 ledger

4x4 posts

$\frac{3}{8}$x1$\frac{1}{2}$-inch cedar or redwood lath

1x2 door stop and trim

HARDWARE

Masonry anchors for lag screws

Galvanized nails

Outdoor screws

Galvanized lag screws and washers

Optional: metal framing connectors and fasteners

OTHER

Roof panels (fiberglass or similar material) and proprietary nails

Contoured support molding for roof panels

Foam weatherstripping

Screening and staples

Screen door, hinges, and latch

Paint, stain, or wood preservative

use painted plywood for the exposed ceiling; for a more sophisticated look, use a layer of beadboard, tongue-and-groove boards, or kerfed plywood siding atop the rafters and under the roof deck.

building a screened-deck addition

As with a porch or patio, screening can transform a deck into a true outdoor room you can use day and night during warm and temperate months.

While an existing deck may be able to handle a very lightweight enclosure, a more substantial structure, such as this one, requires that the deck be designed to support it.

In this project, we provide instructions for constructing and enclosing the deck. Consult your building department early on when contemplating a project such as this. Local codes vary considerably, and some details shown here may not pass muster in your area.

DESIGN DETAILS

Although plain, the open gable in this plan lends itself to a variety of decorative treatments: fanned braces, Victorian gingerbread, and the like. Check your local building-supply stores for prefabricated decorative millwork.

The following instructions are for an easy, inexpensive screening application, but you might want to consider installing the screens in removable frames (see page 40) so you will have the flexibility of replacing them with glass- or plastic-paneled frames to extend use of the room to three seasons.

As shown, screened decks look more finished when their underpinnings are hidden. Choose from lattice panels, tongue-and-groove siding, or 1-by boards to create a skirt for the deck. For ease of installation and minimal expense,

BUILDING NOTES

The pier foundation shown meets most codes; check that the size and spacing of the piers meets with local approval. Deck joists are 2 by 6 on 12-inch centers, with doubled 2-by-8 beams. This "tight" specification allows for minimal thickness of the support members and for a low deck; it also allows for laying the decking diagonally and/or using composite members. However, if your deck will be more than 3 feet above ground and you prefer to lay the decking straight, you can use 2-by-8 joists on 24-inch centers, which will save you time and money. Also, using doubled 2-by-10 or doubled 2-by-12 beams may permit you to reduce the number of piers.

This deck does not depend on the house for support. Instead, a row of footings at the rear supports the structure; a rear rim joist fastened to the house supports the short roof and floor cantilevers. In some cases, the rear footings could be omitted and the deck supported by a ledger attached to the house.

For appearance, the beams sit in notches in 6-by-6 support posts. If you'll be adding skirting to hide the under-deck area, you can save time and money by sub-stituting 4-by-4 posts and metal post-top beam carriers.

STEP-BY-STEP GUIDE

1 **Begin by installing** the pier footings, spaced according to your approved plans, following the instructions on page 101. Screw the 2-by-2 ledger strip to the rear-rim-joist stock with 2½-inch out-door screws, and cut both pieces to length. The end joists will cover the cut ends of the rear rim joist, so the length of the rear rim joist should be equal to the frame width minus two joist thicknesses. Level and mount this assembly to

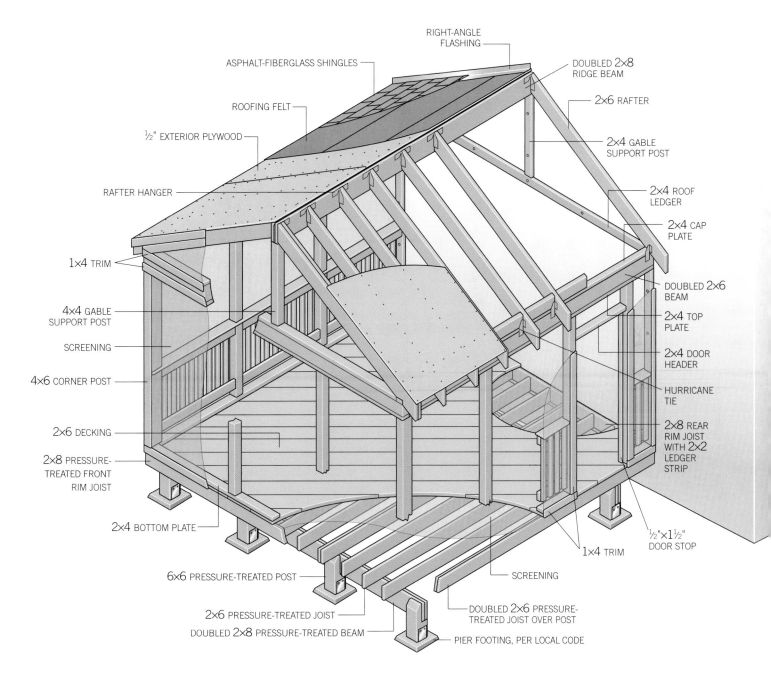

RIGHT-ANGLE FLASHING

ASPHALT-FIBERGLASS SHINGLES

ROOFING FELT

½" EXTERIOR PLYWOOD

RAFTER HANGER

1×4 TRIM

4×4 GABLE SUPPORT POST

SCREENING

4×6 CORNER POST

2×6 DECKING

2×8 PRESSURE-TREATED FRONT RIM JOIST

2×4 BOTTOM PLATE

6×6 PRESSURE-TREATED POST

2×6 PRESSURE-TREATED JOIST

DOUBLED 2×8 PRESSURE-TREATED BEAM

DOUBLED 2×8 RIDGE BEAM

2×6 RAFTER

2×4 GABLE SUPPORT POST

2×4 ROOF LEDGER

2×4 CAP PLATE

DOUBLED 2×6 BEAM

2×4 TOP PLATE

2×4 DOOR HEADER

HURRICANE TIE

2×8 REAR RIM JOIST WITH 2×2 LEDGER STRIP

½"×1½" DOOR STOP

1×4 TRIM

SCREENING

DOUBLED 2×6 PRESSURE-TREATED JOIST OVER POST

PIER FOOTING, PER LOCAL CODE

the house framing, using ½-inch lag screws that, with washers, are long enough to penetrate the wall framing by at least 2 inches. Insert two washers between the joist and the house exterior and a washer under the head of each screw. Mark the end-joist locations on the rear rim joist. Now, cut the front rim joist to the length of the rear rim joist plus two joist thicknesses. Mark the end-joist locations on this member, too.

2 **Mark and cut** the 6-by-6 support posts, following the directions on pages 108–109. Also cut the notches and bevels for the beams. If you're mounting beams atop 4-by-4 posts, you can permanently mount the posts on the footings, subtract the beam depth from the joist height, and cut the posts to length without having to take them down.

3 **Cut two lengths** of 2 by 8 for each beam, add 4-inch-wide ½-inch plywood spacers every foot, and nail the boards and spacers together with 12d nails. Cut the beams a few inches long so you can shift the joists slightly to square up the frame, if necessary. Cut the plywood spacers in the shape of fence pickets, and fasten them with their points up. Mount the beams, crown sides up, in the post notches, and fasten them with ½-inch lag screws and washers (or mount them atop 4-by-4 posts with metal post-top beam carriers and nails or screws).

PLAN VIEW

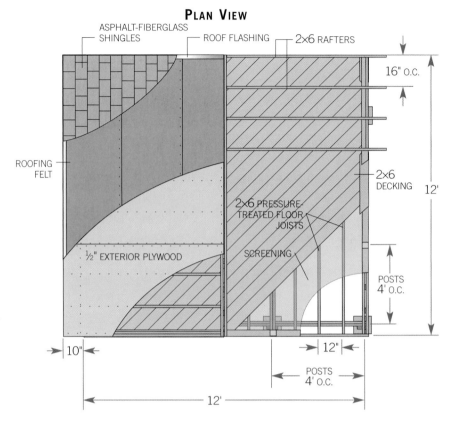

FRONT ELEVATION VIEW

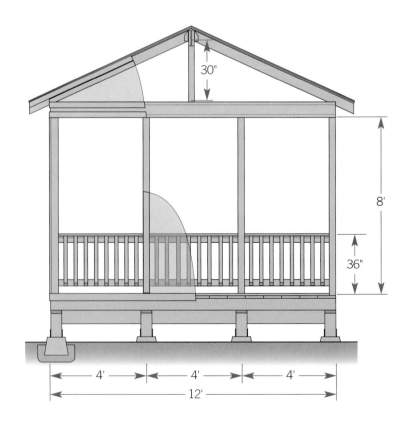

4 **Rest the untrimmed** end joists on the beams, and nail them to the rear-rim-joist ends with three 12d nails. Lay the front rim joist flat across the side joists near their ends. Square up the frame, and attach the joists to the beams. Though codes allow toenailing with three 8d or 10d nails, seismic or hurricane ties—easier to install and stronger—are preferable, especially where the hardware won't show. Install the remaining untrimmed joists (you can use the marks on the front rim joist as a guide). Toenail the ends of these joists to the rear rim joist with two pairs of 10d nails. (Note that the side joists are doubled, as are the joists that intersect the front

posts.) Finally, snap a chalk line to mark the joists for trimming. Extend the line down the face of each joist. Cut the joists to length, and then nail the front rim joist to each joist end with three 12d nails.

5 **Staple a layer** of screening to the joists, and then install the 2-by-6 decking. Lay the decking diagonally, fastening with coated outdoor screws that match the wood. Make 45-degree cuts where deck boards abut the house, and leave a ¼-inch gap. Allow the boards to run a few inches long on the other three sides of the framing. Space screws 1 inch in from the board edge. Use two screws at each joist intersection,

driving the heads flush with the surface. Use an 8d common nail as a spacer between dry boards; butt green boards together. Use a straightedge or snap a chalk line to align the screws. After you fasten the decking, snap chalk lines and cut the decking flush with the joists beneath. Sand the edges.

6 **Measure, cut, and assemble** the side-wall members flat on the deck. Cut the 2-by-4 bottom plates to run from the house to the far edges of the 4-by-6 outer corner posts, minus ⅜ inch for spacers and weatherstripping at the house. Cut the 2-by-4 top plates to run from the house to within 3½ inches of the far edges of the corner posts (the gap will be filled by the gable wall's top plate), minus the same ⅜ inch. Drill ½-inch pilot holes in the inner corner posts for the lag screws that will fasten the posts to the house. Counterbore for the washers. Mark the post locations on the plates. Making sure they are square, nail the plates to the posts with two or three 12d nails at each intersection.

7 **Erect and fasten** each wall in turn, about ⅜ inch away from the house and so the bottom plates are flush with the deck edges. Plumb each wall, and then screw them to the house framing with ½-inch lag screws that, with two washers each, are long enough to penetrate the wall framing by 2 inches. Nail the bot-

SIDE ELEVATION VIEW

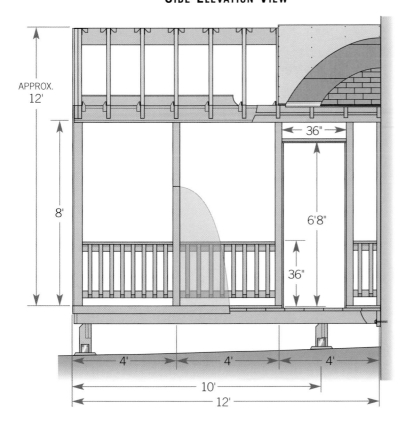

APPROX. 12'

8'

36"

6'8"

36"

4'   4'   4'

10'

12'

tom plates to the deck with 12d nails. Plumb and brace the outer corners with temporary diagonal braces attached to the 4-by-6 posts and the front rim joist. Trim away the sill in the door opening.

8 **Measure, cut, and assemble** the gable-end wall but not the gable support post. Measure and cut the bottom plate to run between the side-wall plates, and measure and cut the top plate to extend to the outer edges of the side-wall plates. Erect this wall with the aid of helpers, lifting it up and over the side walls' top plates so that its plate engages the gap atop the corner posts. Plumb the wall, and then nail the bottom plate to the deck and the top plate to the corner posts with 12d nails. Remove the braces.

9 **Cut the roof beams,** made from paired 2 by 6s separated by $\frac{1}{2}$-inch plywood spacers 12 inches on center, to run the full length of the side walls. Toenail the beams to the top plates with 12d nails. Cut the gable roof beam to fit between the side roof beams, and toenail it in place. Cut a 2-by-4 cap plate to run the full width of the gable end, and nail it on with 12d nails. Finally, cut two 2-by-4 cap plates to run atop the side walls from the gable-end cap plate to the house. Nail them on with 12d nails. Cut the 2-by-4 ledger, and place it against the house, flush with the top edges of the side walls' cap plates. Drive

$\frac{1}{2}$-inch lag screws through the ledger into the house framing.

10 **Cut a 30-inch-long** 4-by-4 gable-end support post and a 2-by-4 rear gable support post. Attach the 4 by 4 to the center of the gable's cap plate, driving two pairs of $3\frac{1}{2}$-inch outdoor screws diagonally into pilot holes. Attach the 2 by 4, centered on the roof ledger, to the house using $3\frac{1}{2}$-inch outdoor screws. Measure from the house wall to the top of the gable post, and then cut two 2-by-8 ridge beams to this measurement. Separate these boards with $\frac{1}{2}$-inch plywood spacers 12 inches on center, and nail the boards together with 12d nails. Lay out and mark the rafter locations on this ridge beam. With a helper, place the beam atop the support posts. Attach it at the gable end with $3\frac{1}{2}$-inch outdoor screws, driven diagonally, and at the house end with a pair of screws driven into the post and a pair driven into the house wall.

11 **Nail a rafter** hanger at the rafter mark on the far end of the beam. With a helper, take a piece of 2-by-6 rafter stock and place it in the hanger; measure for the diagonal cut at the ridge and the bird's-mouth cut at the cap plate. Make the cuts, and then test for fit. Make adjustments until the rafter fits on both ends in all locations. Use this rafter as a template to mark and cut the other rafters, and make slight adjustments

where necessary. Attach the rafters using rafter hangers at the ridge beam and rafter ties at the roof beams.

12 **Cut and nail** $\frac{1}{2}$-inch plywood to the rafters. Add a layer of 15-pound roofing felt per the manufacturer's specifications. Flash the house-roof connection with right-angle flashing, and flash the roof as discussed on page 119. Follow with shingles, installing according to the manufacturer's specifications (also see pages 122–123). Install the upper 1-by-4 trim, butting it against the rafter tails on the sides and across the gable front. Nail the trim on with 8d galvanized finish nails.

13 **Make the railing** panels from 2-by-2 balusters attached to 2-by-4 top and bottom rails with $2\frac{1}{2}$-inch outdoor screws. A 1-by-6 cap, notched to go around the posts, finishes off the railings. Cut and install the 2 by 4s first, attaching them to the inner sides of the posts and to each other at the outer corners. Then attach the balusters, driving two screws through each end of the 2 by 2s into the 2 by 4s. Finish with the notched cap.

14 **To complete** your screened room, add the screening (see page 40). Cap the screens with the prefinished 1-by-4 trim (screw the trim in place to facilitate repairs). Hang the door as described on pages 74–75.

LOWER CORNER DETAIL

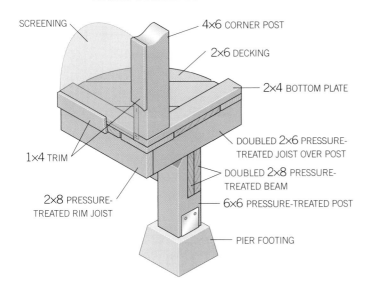

SCREENING

4×6 CORNER POST

2×6 DECKING

2×4 BOTTOM PLATE

1×4 TRIM

DOUBLED 2×6 PRESSURE-TREATED JOIST OVER POST

DOUBLED 2×8 PRESSURE-TREATED BEAM

6×6 PRESSURE-TREATED POST

2×8 PRESSURE-TREATED RIM JOIST

PIER FOOTING

UPPER CORNER DETAIL

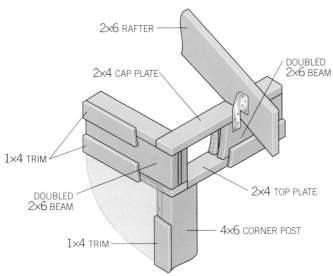

2×6 RAFTER

2×4 CAP PLATE

DOUBLED 2×6 BEAM

1×4 TRIM

2×4 TOP PLATE

DOUBLED 2×6 BEAM

4×6 CORNER POST

1×4 TRIM

RAILING DETAIL

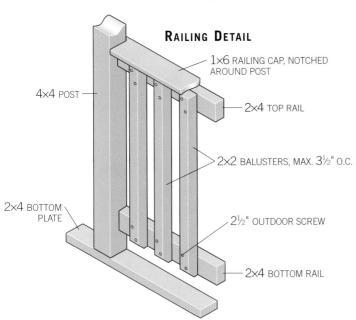

1×6 RAILING CAP, NOTCHED AROUND POST

4×4 POST

2×4 TOP RAIL

2×2 BALUSTERS, MAX. 3½" O.C.

2×4 BOTTOM PLATE

2½" OUTDOOR SCREW

2×4 BOTTOM RAIL

MATERIALS CHECKLIST

LUMBER

2x2 pressure-treated rear-rim-joist ledger

2x2 balusters

2x4 framing

2x6 pressure-treated joists

2x6 beams (doubled)

2x6 decking

2x6 rafters

2x8 pressure-treated rim joists

2x8 pressure-treated beams (doubled)

2x8 ridge beam (doubled)

6x6 pressure-treated posts

4x6 posts

4x4 interior and gable support posts

½-inch exterior plywood

1x4 trim

1x6 railing caps

½x1½-inch door stops

HARDWARE

10d and 12d galvanized nails

8d galvanized finish nails

2½- and 3½-inch outdoor screws

Galvanized lag screws and washers

Metal framing connectors and fasteners

Flashing for ledger

Screening and staples

OTHER

Concrete, #4 rebar, and form lumber for footings

Pier footings

15-pound roofing felt

Asphalt-fiberglass shingles and metal roof flashing

Screen door, hinges, and latch

Foam weatherstripping

Paint, stain, or wood preservative

adding on a screened room

This handsome screened room, which harmonizes with the house's style and form, is designed as a three-season addition.

This screened-room addition features a substantial roof structure set atop a simple, graceful post-and-beam frame. A pediment in the Colonial style is punctuated by a traditional gable window. The classic design makes the room look like it's always been there. Fitted with removable glass, this add-on will function like any other room in the house.

DESIGN DETAILS

The Colonial gable shown is easy to adapt to other styles, from ranch to Victorian to Craftsman. It can be dressed up with dentil molding or left open in the manner of the screened-deck addition on page 48. The round window is easily changed out with other shapes, a simple vent, or nothing at all. The roof pitch matches that of the house; it should be adapted if your house's roofline is different. For a seamless appearance, the same applies to materials and colors.

The design assumes a door centered on the front gable and a complementary doorway into the house, but you may relocate these to fit your situation. Slab height should be set so there's only a step or two from house to room; a box step can be fastened to the slab with masonry anchors. The stairs into the yard can be any kind, from simple boards to masonry.

BUILDING NOTES

The slab foundation shown will meet code in most municipalities, but it's always safest to check with your local building department.

Given a smooth, textured, or stained surface, the slab itself can serve as the room's floor. Or, the slab can be covered with tile, brick, or other paver units. Allow for the thickness of any paver units when setting the slab height so the floor won't block the house door. Include the stair foundation in your slab pour.

The room's slab drains by means of scuppers (grooves) cut across the undersides of the sills. If tile or other masonry flooring will sit on top of the slab, either use mortarless units or omit the mortar joints near the scuppers to permit drainage.

The back-wall support assumes no weight-bearing attachment to the house. If you can gain some support from your house—by lagscrewing into the second-floor rim

The addition of this screened entry enhances the house's entire look. The round center window balances out the sharp angles of the facade. Design: Robert Orr Architects

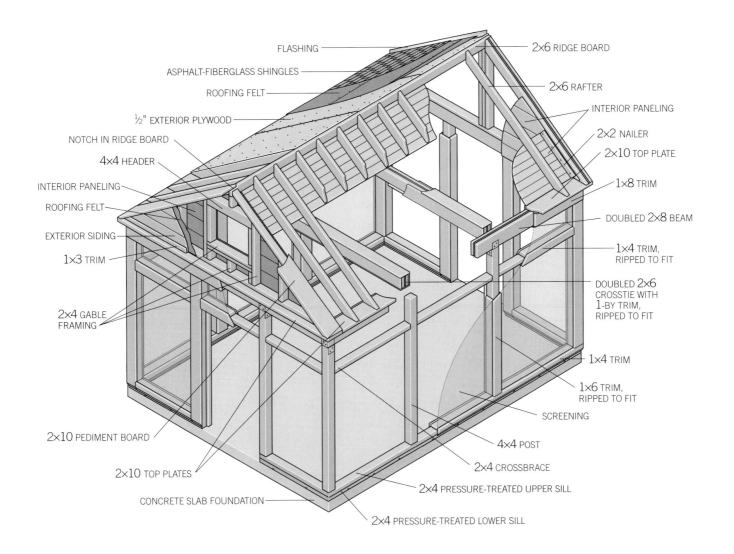

FLASHING

ASPHALT-FIBERGLASS SHINGLES

ROOFING FELT

½" EXTERIOR PLYWOOD

NOTCH IN RIDGE BOARD

4×4 HEADER

INTERIOR PANELING

ROOFING FELT

EXTERIOR SIDING

1×3 TRIM

2×4 GABLE FRAMING

2×10 PEDIMENT BOARD

2×10 TOP PLATES

CONCRETE SLAB FOUNDATION

2×6 RIDGE BOARD

2×6 RAFTER

INTERIOR PANELING

2×2 NAILER

2×10 TOP PLATE

1×8 TRIM

DOUBLED 2×8 BEAM

1×4 TRIM, RIPPED TO FIT

DOUBLED 2×6 CROSSTIE WITH 1-BY TRIM, RIPPED TO FIT

1×4 TRIM

1×6 TRIM, RIPPED TO FIT

SCREENING

4×4 POST

2×4 CROSSBRACE

2×4 PRESSURE-TREATED UPPER SILL

2×4 PRESSURE-TREATED LOWER SILL

joist, for example—you may be able to omit some of the rear framing shown here. Work with your building department to determine your options.

STEP-BY-STEP GUIDE

1 **Locate, measure,** and excavate for the foundation. Stake form boards around the excavation to create an integral slab, as shown on page 103, at least 6 inches above grade. Arrange the forms to allow for a drainage slope of ¼-inch per foot from the house outward. Place, rake, and level a gravel bed 4 to 6 inches deep. Add a layer of 6-mil vapor barrier. Hold it in place with a few handfuls of gravel, taking care not to perforate it.

2 **Add steel reinforcing bar** and 6-inch, 10-10 welded-steel mesh to reinforce the slab, and then pour and finish the concrete, as shown on pages 102–103. Sink anchor bolts in the fresh concrete where indicated. (Note that there are no anchor bolts in the doorway section.) Cover the finished slab, or keep it damp for a day or two after finishing, and then strip

the forms. Once the slab has cured, color it with concrete stain, if desired. Cut the front, rear, and side lower sills from pressure-treated lumber, and cut the ¾-by-¾-inch scuppers across their undersides. Square up the sills, and fasten them with the anchor bolts, countersinking the nuts and washers. Using a hack saw or bolt-cutters, cut the bolts flush with the tops of the sills.

3 **Measure, cut, and assemble** the side walls flat on the slab, making sure to allow for the slope of the slab when you cut the posts. For

TOP PLAN VIEW

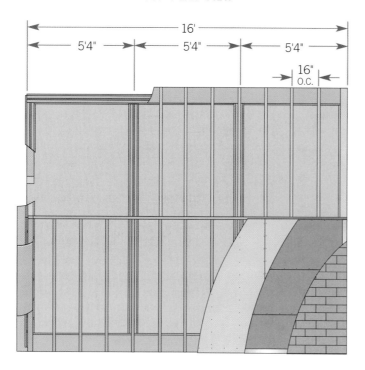

16'

5'4" · 5'4" · 5'4"

16" O.C.

SIDE ELEVATION VIEW

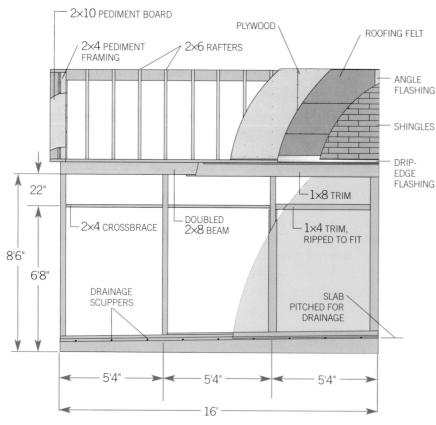

2×10 PEDIMENT BOARD

PLYWOOD

ROOFING FELT

2×4 PEDIMENT FRAMING

2×6 RAFTERS

ANGLE FLASHING

SHINGLES

DRIP-EDGE FLASHING

1×8 TRIM

22"

2×4 CROSSBRACE

DOUBLED 2×8 BEAM

1×4 TRIM, RIPPED TO FIT

8'6"

6'8"

DRAINAGE SCUPPERS

SLAB PITCHED FOR DRAINAGE

5'4" · 5'4" · 5'4"

16'

each wall, include the 2-by-4 pressure-treated upper sills that will sit on the sills already bolted to the slab, the 4-by-4 posts, the 2-by-4 horizontal braces, and the doubled 2-by-8 beams with $\frac{1}{2}$-inch plywood spacers. Do not include the top plates. Gang-cut all pieces so that both walls will be identical. If necessary, drill holes in the upper sills for the anchor bolts. For speed and accuracy, place the sills and beams together and mark the post locations on them. Make sure the assemblies are square before nailing or screwing them together with metal framing connectors.

4 **With several helpers,** erect, align, and nail each side wall to the pressure-treated bottom sills. Plumb and brace the outer corners with temporary diagonal braces attached to the corner posts and the gable-end sills. Plumb the walls at the house end, and then screw them to the house framing with $\frac{1}{2}$-inch lag screws, counterbored into the rear posts.

5 **Measure and cut** the interior posts for both gable ends; add post caps, and nail the posts to the upper sills. Erect each assembly, and then align, plumb, and nail each upper sill to each lower sill. Check again that the outer posts are square and plumb, and then measure for the front and rear beams. If you haven't already done so, cut and assemble the beams, and, with helpers, lift them into place. Nail the post caps to the beams, toenail the beam ends to the side-wall beams with 16d nails, and reinforce the connection with angle brackets (as shown in the detail on page 59). Measure, cut, and attach the 2-by-10 top plates to the three exterior walls with 12d nails. Nail the 1-by-3 trim beneath the plates using 4d nails.

6 **Cut two 2 by 4s** to 46½ inches. These will serve as temporary braces for the ridge board and determine its height. First, mark the center of the rear top plate. Place one 2 by 4 on edge along the rear top plate so its centerline aligns with the mark on the plate. Plumb the 2 by 4, and toenail its top to the house. Similarly, mount

and plumb the other 2 by 4 in the center of the front gable, holding it in place vertically with temporary braces, and toenail it to the top plate. Make sure the braces are robust because they must temporarily support the ridge board while you take rafter and gable-frame measurements.

7 **Choose a straight** 16-foot-long 2 by 6, and, with helpers, mount it to the top of the 2-by-4 supports. Screw the ridge board in place temporarily using scrap wood to bridge the 2 by 4s and the ridge board. With the ridge board temporarily mounted, measure and cut a master rafter from an 8-foot-long 2 by 6. Cut it to extend from the ridge to the outer edge of the 2-by-10 plate.

FRONT ELEVATION VIEW

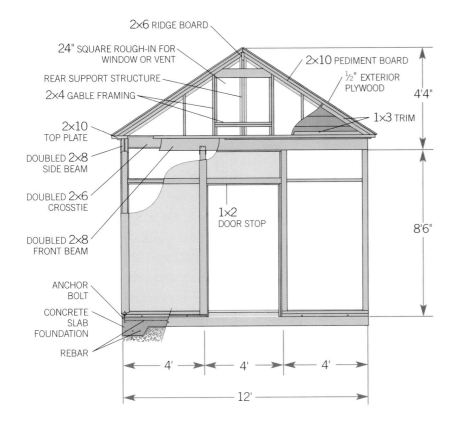

2×6 RIDGE BOARD

24" SQUARE ROUGH-IN FOR WINDOW OR VENT

REAR SUPPORT STRUCTURE

2×4 GABLE FRAMING

2×10 TOP PLATE

DOUBLED 2×8 SIDE BEAM

DOUBLED 2×6 CROSSTIE

DOUBLED 2×8 FRONT BEAM

ANCHOR BOLT

CONCRETE SLAB FOUNDATION

REBAR

2×10 PEDIMENT BOARD

½" EXTERIOR PLYWOOD

1×3 TRIM

1×2 DOOR STOP

4'4"

8'6"

4'   4'   4'

12'

MATERIALS CHECKLIST

LUMBER

2x4 pressure-treated sills

2x4 framing

4x4 posts and header

2x8 beams (doubled)

2x10 top plates and pediments

2x6 rafters, crossties, and ridge board

1x3, 1x4, 1x6, 1x8, and 1x12 trim

1x2 door stops

2x2 nailers

½-inch exterior plywood

6-inch cedar or redwood shiplap or tongue-and-groove siding

Tongue-and-groove or beadboard interior paneling

HARDWARE

½-inch anchor bolts, washers, and nuts

Galvanized nails

4d galvanized finish nails

Outdoor screws

Galvanized lag screws and washers

Metal framing connectors and fasteners

Screening and staples

OTHER

Concrete, #4 rebar, and form lumber for foundation

Gravel

6-mil vapor barrier

6-inch, 10-10 welded-steel mesh

15-pound roofing felt

Roof flashing

Asphalt-fiberglass shingles

Prefabricated gable window or vent

Exterior caulk

Paint, stain, or wood preservative

Two screen doors, hinges, and latches

When you're satisfied with its accuracy, use this master rafter as a template to mark and cut the remaining rafters.

8 **Measure** for the front-gable framing. The top surfaces of the angled members should intersect the ridge board at just over 4 feet up from the top plate, but it's best to take this measurement on site rather than rely on the plans. An easy way to do this is to take a 2-by scrap, with one end cut to the rafter–ridge board angle, and hold it against the front of the ridge board at its vertical center. Mark the point where the lower edge of the 2-by intersects the ridge board; this locates the upper edge of the framing. Using a try square, extend this mark across the ridge board. Next, hold a scrap of 2-by, with one end cut at the rafter-to-plate angle, at the edge of each side plate. Mark the inner edge on the side plates to locate the sideward extension of these gable members. The measurement between the marks on the ridge board and side plates is the length of these gable-frame members. Finally, remove the ridge board.

9 **Back on the ground,** cut the 2-by-4 gable-frame members, and assemble them with 12d nails. Note that this project calls for a 24-inch rough-in opening for the window or vent, but the size of this opening can be easily adjusted. With helpers, lift the gable

frame into position and nail it to the top plate with 12d nails, making sure it's plumb and centered on the rear edge of the front wall. Remount the ridge board, and fasten it permanently at each end with 12d nails. At the house end, add the paired rafters with $\frac{1}{2}$-inch plywood spacers and the extra 2-by-4 supports.

10 **Notch the front** of the ridge board to clear the 2-by-10 top pediment members. Measure and cut these members from 8-foot-long 2 by 10s. Nail them to the framing and to the 2-by-10 front top plates. From 12-foot-long 2-by-6 stock, measure and cut the crossties. Assemble the ties with $\frac{1}{2}$-inch plywood spacers, and then nail them in place using 4-by-6 joist hangers and proprietary nails. Measure and mark the ridge board and side plates for the remaining rafters, and nail them in place with 12d nails.

11 **Cut and nail** $\frac{1}{2}$-inch plywood to the rafters and upper pediment members using 8d nails. Follow with roofing felt. Flash the house-roof connection with right-angle flashing. Also flash the roof edges. Install the shingles according to the manufacturer's specifications. Mount and flash the window or vent unit in the front gable according to the manufacturer's instructions. Add the exterior tongue-and-groove or shiplap siding on the front-gable framing, butting it against the 2 by 10s and

nailing it with 4d galvanized finish nails. Caulk these connections, and then cut and add the 1-by-3 trim and any trim that came with the window or vent. Caulk this trim to seal out moisture.

12 **Trim** the finished frame, working from the beams down. Start with the 1-by-4 trim under the beams, and then cut and fit the 1-by-8 trim outside and the $9\frac{3}{4}$-inch trim inside (ripped from 1-by-12 stock). Mount all interior trim with 4d finish nails, but don't mount the exterior trim yet (you'll install it once the screens are up). Start the crosstie cladding with 1 by 6s and the post cladding with 1 by 4s, and cap off with 5-inch trim ripped from 1-by-6 stock. Finish the gable interiors with tongue-and-groove (or beadboard) paneling. Add 2-by-2 nailers to the gables where shown, and nail paneling to the nailers and rafters with 4d finish nails. Nail the 1-by-2 door stops in place with 4d finish nails.

13 **To complete** the screened room, paint or stain all exposed wood, plus the still-unmounted exterior trim. Stretch the screening in place, and staple it to the outside of the framing (for more about techniques for installing screening, see page 40). Cap the screens by screwing the prefinished trim in place with color-coated outdoor screws to allow for easy repairs. Hang the screen door, and fit the latch.

Ridge Detail

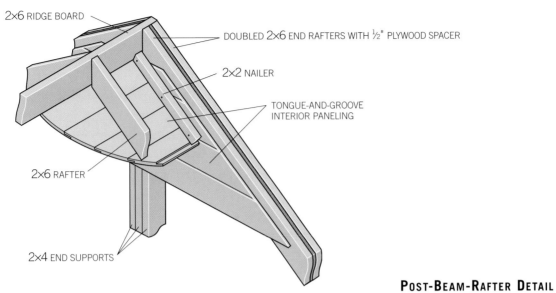

2×6 RIDGE BOARD

DOUBLED 2×6 END RAFTERS WITH ½" PLYWOOD SPACER

2×2 NAILER

TONGUE-AND-GROOVE INTERIOR PANELING

2×6 RAFTER

2×4 END SUPPORTS

Post-Beam-Rafter Detail

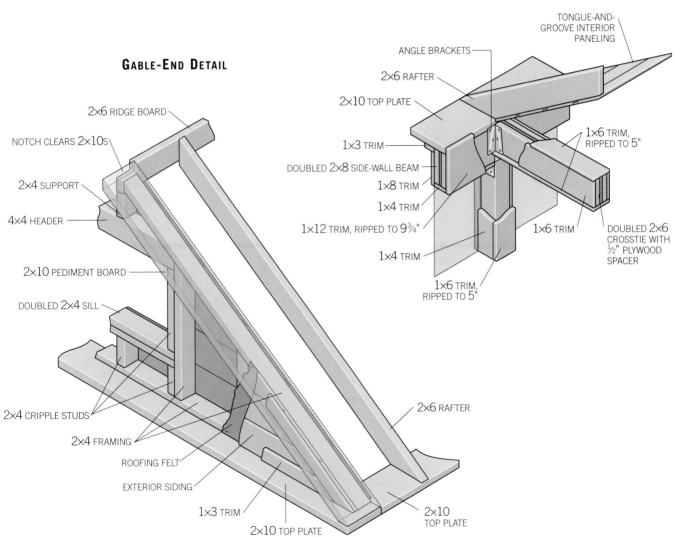

TONGUE-AND-GROOVE INTERIOR PANELING

ANGLE BRACKETS

2×6 RAFTER

2×10 TOP PLATE

1×3 TRIM

DOUBLED 2×8 SIDE-WALL BEAM

1×8 TRIM

1×4 TRIM

1×12 TRIM, RIPPED TO 9¾"

1×4 TRIM

1×6 TRIM, RIPPED TO 5"

1×6 TRIM, RIPPED TO 5"

1×6 TRIM

DOUBLED 2×6 CROSSTIE WITH ½" PLYWOOD SPACER

Gable-End Detail

2×6 RIDGE BOARD

NOTCH CLEARS 2×10s

2×4 SUPPORT

4×4 HEADER

2×10 PEDIMENT BOARD

DOUBLED 2×4 SILL

2×4 CRIPPLE STUDS

2×4 FRAMING

ROOFING FELT

EXTERIOR SIDING

1×3 TRIM

2×10 TOP PLATE

2×6 RAFTER

2×10 TOP PLATE

assembling a kit gazebo

Does a screened gazebo seem like the perfect improvement for your yard? If it does, consider the type that's sold as a kit.

Cutting compound angles, shaping wood, and making difficult joints are just a few of the tasks involved in building a custom gazebo. Thankfully, several quality woodworking companies produce gazebo kits—many available with screens. With these, most of the difficult work is already done—you just provide the spot, assemble the parts, and enjoy the results.

BUILDING NOTES

Nearly all gazebo kits come with complete instructions for assembly; be sure to follow them implicitly. The directions given here are for the Dalton Pavilions gazebo shown below. They are specific to this project so they will not be applicable to other models or other manufacturers' gazebos.

With most kits, components are typically numbered or coded to correspond with diagrams and assembly directions. Kits also include screws, bolts, nails, and various connection brackets and plates. Foundation materials are not included.

Because some of the components are heavy or awkward to handle, you'll need a helper. In fact, a large gazebo may require two helpers when it's time to lift the roof components.

Before you begin assembly, you'll need to cast a concrete foundation according to the manufacturer's directions. Proper layout of the foundation piers is critical because the kit's components are sized to fit this layout.

Pour 12-inch concrete piers below grade in accordance with local code requirements. For more about casting a foundation, see pages 102–103.

STEP-BY-STEP GUIDE

1 **Drill in masonry anchors** and lag-screw the metal center plate to the foundation pier at the center of the layout. The octagon's points should be in line with the outer piers. Next, position the eight floor joists and attach them to the center plate using bolts, nuts, and washers. Just finger-tighten the nuts for now. Sight down each joist to make sure it lines up with its opposite joist.

2 **Connect the joist ends** with skirt boards. Make the connections with threaded rods, washers, nuts,

This simple kit-built screened gazebo serves as a poolside cabana at the water's edge. Design: Dalton Pavilions

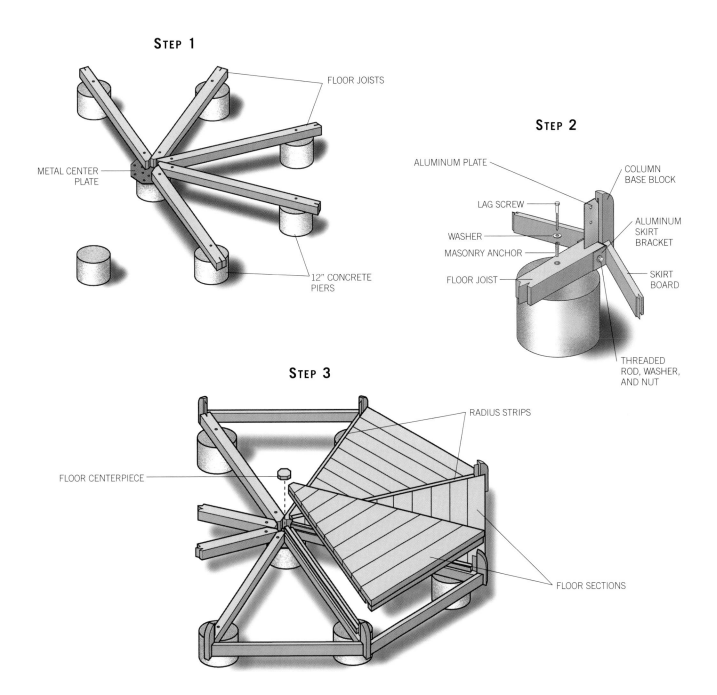

STEP 1

FLOOR JOISTS

METAL CENTER PLATE

12" CONCRETE PIERS

STEP 2

ALUMINUM PLATE

LAG SCREW

WASHER

MASONRY ANCHOR

FLOOR JOIST

COLUMN BASE BLOCK

ALUMINUM SKIRT BRACKET

SKIRT BOARD

THREADED ROD, WASHER, AND NUT

STEP 3

FLOOR CENTERPIECE

RADIUS STRIPS

FLOOR SECTIONS

aluminum skirt brackets, and column base blocks as shown at top right. Make sure the top edges of the skirt boards sit flush with the tops of the floor joists. Finger-tighten a nut (with a washer) at each end of each threaded rod. Now tighten the nuts at the center plate. Finish by bolting the floor joists to the anchors in the concrete piers using lag screws.

3 **To install the floor,** line up each section's side edges between two floor joists, and place the back edge snug against the column base blocks. Before screwing down the sections, insert radius strips between them, facing the rabbeted edges upward. Using a mallet, tap the floor sections toward the centerpiece until the fit is tight and the outer edges of the floor

nailers are even. Then use galvanized screws to fasten the floor sections to the joists. Use trim screws to fasten the radius strips to the floor centerpiece.

4 **Secure the columns** to the base blocks with bolts, washers, and nuts, positioning the molded sides outward. Attach the upper column bands at the top of the columns using eye bolts and eye-bolt pins. Just finger-tighten the nuts until you place all of the upper column bands. Then, tighten the nuts, alternating between the right and left nuts on each column. Screw the inside trim blocks in place with trim screws.

5 Install the side panels by positioning each panel so it has equal margins on each side and by screwing it to the columns.

6 Begin installing the rafters by laying the pair of truss rafters on a flat, level surface and positioning the plastic truss strap straight. Fit the rafter center post between the rafter ends, even with their tops, and secure it with screws. With a helper, slide the truss into the slots at the tops of two opposite columns. Be sure the bird's-mouth cuts seat fully and fit against the trim blocks. Then screw the rafters in place. With one person positioned near the center, screw the remaining rafters in place.

7 Install a roof support band or a screen band, depending on the size and type of your gazebo, between the rafters around the perimeter. Keep the bands flush with the top edge of the rafters, and screw them in place.

8 Center the roof sections over the rafters, and secure them by driving screws through predrilled holes. Beginning at the eaves line, install the hip shingles, starting with a short one, continuing up the roof with long ones, and finishing at the peak with short ones. Secure the shingles with galvanized nails; place the nails where overlapping shingles will cover them.

9 Place the peak cap on top so its threaded rod projects through the roof's center. Screw down the finial, securing it against the peak cap. If you're installing a small cupola, use a longer threaded rod and place the cupola's body between the roof and the peak cap.

10 Position and fasten the handrails to the columns with screws, if your gazebo comes with open panels. Secure the alu-

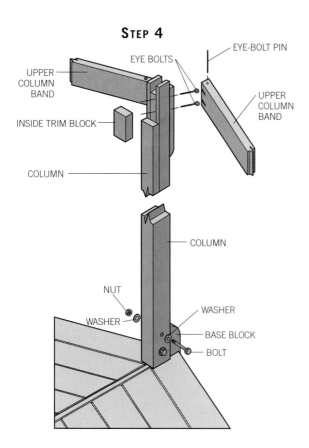

STEP 4

EYE BOLTS
EYE-BOLT PIN
UPPER COLUMN BAND
UPPER COLUMN BAND
INSIDE TRIM BLOCK
COLUMN
COLUMN
NUT
WASHER
WASHER
BASE BLOCK
BOLT

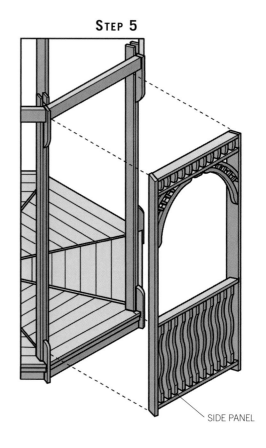

STEP 5

SIDE PANEL

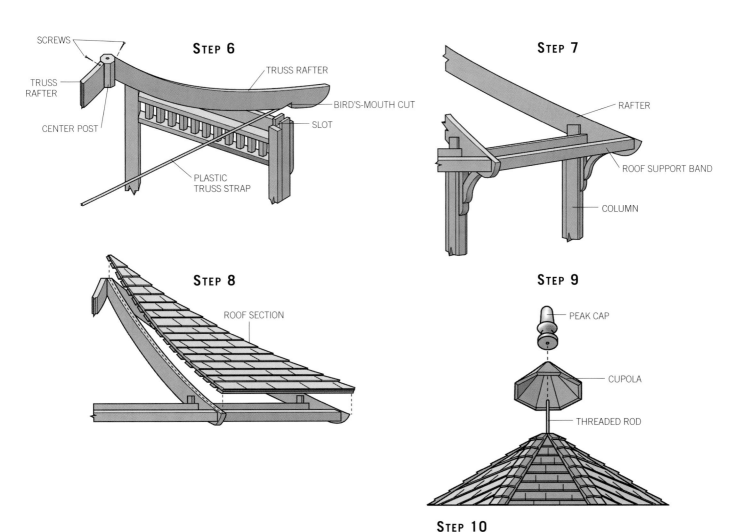

STEP 6

SCREWS

TRUSS RAFTER

TRUSS RAFTER

CENTER POST

PLASTIC TRUSS STRAP

BIRD'S-MOUTH CUT

SLOT

STEP 7

RAFTER

ROOF SUPPORT BAND

COLUMN

STEP 8

ROOF SECTION

STEP 9

PEAK CAP

CUPOLA

THREADED ROD

STEP 10

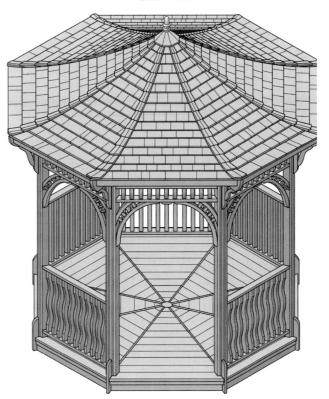

minum-framed screen panels to the inside edges of the door panel and side panels with the provided #10x1-inch stainless-steel screws. This allows for easy removal for repairs. The gazebo's door is pre-hung within the entrance panel. Make sure the edge clearances are sufficient and consistent before screwing the jambs to the columns. Install the door latch following the manufacturer's instructions. Set any exposed nailheads beneath the surface, and fill the holes with matching wood filler. Cut and remove the plastic truss strap.

building a garden room

Set apart from the house, this screened garden room can serve as a private getaway or a hub for entertaining.

In form, this crisp octagonal garden room is reminiscent of a classic Victorian gazebo, but it cuts a markedly modern profile. Simple yet effective trim frames the handsome reveals that create plays of light on the interior as the sun moves across the sky. The walls are open to breezes, and an acrylic-sheet skylight balances illumination inside. Although it is a major project, the structure is not fussy and has easy-to-understand building directions.

DESIGN DETAILS

The octagonal shape of this structure efficiently creates maximum space within a minimal perimeter. The room provides plenty of area for a dining table and chairs and other furniture. You can scale the room down if you like, but if you decide to scale it up, consult a professional to check that the lumber sizes are sufficient. The acrylic-sheet skylight can be located in any section of the roof. In warmer climates, facing it north will minimize heat build-up; in cooler areas, placing it toward the south will maximize warmth.

BUILDING NOTES

The garden room rests on a concrete grade-beam (integral-footing) foundation and slab floor, which are subject to local code requirements. The footing must be set a minimum of 18 inches deep or to the frost line (the depth at which soil freezes in your area). Check with your local building department if you're unsure of your locale's standards.

A great advantage of the framing method used is that seven of the eight wall sections are identical. You can measure the pieces for a single section, use them as guides for the others, and cut them all at one time.

Double doors open wide, inviting guests into this generously sized screened garden room. Architect: Lou Kimball

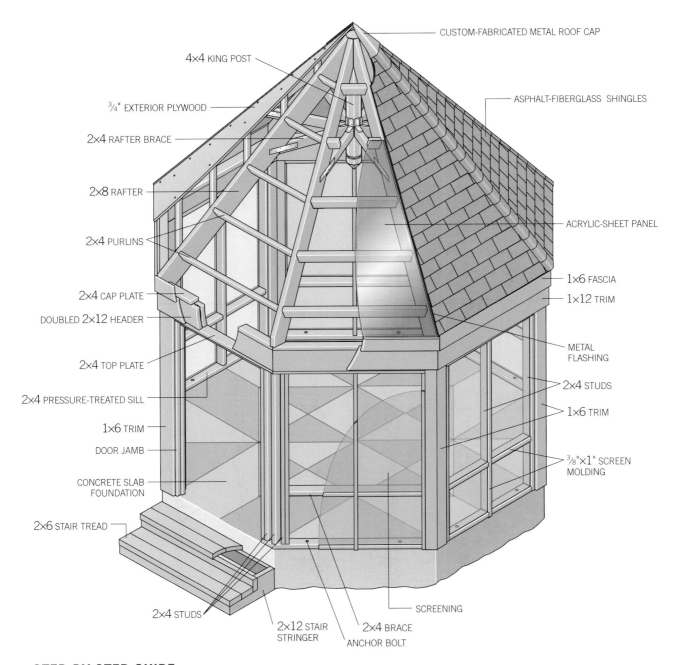

CUSTOM-FABRICATED METAL ROOF CAP

4×4 KING POST

¾" EXTERIOR PLYWOOD

2×4 RAFTER BRACE

2×8 RAFTER

2×4 PURLINS

2×4 CAP PLATE

DOUBLED 2×12 HEADER

2×4 TOP PLATE

2×4 PRESSURE-TREATED SILL

1×6 TRIM

DOOR JAMB

CONCRETE SLAB FOUNDATION

2×6 STAIR TREAD

2×4 STUDS

2×12 STAIR STRINGER

2×4 BRACE

ANCHOR BOLT

SCREENING

ASPHALT-FIBERGLASS SHINGLES

ACRYLIC-SHEET PANEL

1×6 FASCIA

1×12 TRIM

METAL FLASHING

2×4 STUDS

1×6 TRIM

⅜"×1" SCREEN MOLDING

STEP-BY-STEP GUIDE

1 **Locate and measure** for the octagonal foundation, and then dig the foundation trench. Stake form boards around the trench to create a footing that is 18 inches above grade on the outside. Each wall segment should measure 6 feet from corner to corner. Place, rake, and level a gravel bed 6 inches deep so that its top is

6 inches below the form boards. Shape it as shown in the foundation cross section on page 68. Add a layer of 6-mil vapor barrier over the gravel, and hold it in place with a few handfuls of gravel. Be careful not to perforate the barrier—doing so would allow ground water to wick up through the concrete slab.

2 **Add rebar,** and then pour the concrete (see pages 102–103), screeding to create a ¼-inch-per-foot runoff slope from the center to the perimeter. Sink anchor bolts in the fresh concrete where shown; do not place anchor bolts in the doorway section. The slab floor of the garden room shown here has a pattern of scored lines

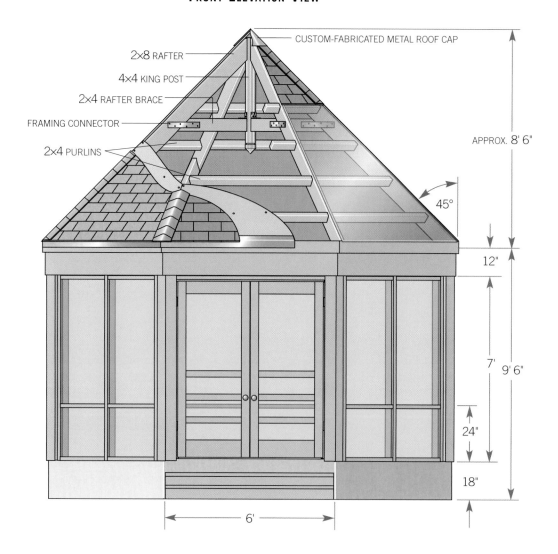

CUSTOM-FABRICATED METAL ROOF CAP

2×8 RAFTER

4×4 KING POST

2×4 RAFTER BRACE

FRAMING CONNECTOR

2×4 PURLINS

APPROX. 8' 6"

45°

12"

7'

9' 6"

24"

18"

6'

that crisscross on 2-foot centers (see the illustration on the facing page). After smoothing the surface with a steel trowel, use a jointing tool to score these lines. Be sure to wait until the concrete is firm enough to support the weight of your body kneeling on long boards (this is how you will be positioned to score the surface). Cover the slab, and keep it damp for a day or two after finishing. Then strip the forms. If you wish, color the slab with concrete stain once it has cured.

3 **To build** the seven identical wall sections, start by cutting the 22½-degree angles at the ends of each 6-foot pressure-treated sill. Cut two ¾-by-¾-inch slots on 2-foot centers across the bottom of each sill for drainage. Using 16d nails, fasten pairs of 81-inch studs at each end of each sill, spacing them in from the ends to leave room for the angled filler studs you'll add later. Fasten a final stud in the center of each section, bracing it with horizontal 2 by 4s fastened with outdoor

screws. Finish with a 2-by-4 top plate. Measure and drill ½-inch holes in each sill, and bolt each wall section to the foundation. Counterbore for the washers and nuts, and cut the bolts off flush with the sill and top plate. Connect the wall sections with angled filler studs screwed in place.

4 **Build the door framing** by nailing pairs of studs to short bottom plates and a full-length top plate. Fasten the door framing in place with angled filler studs as you did

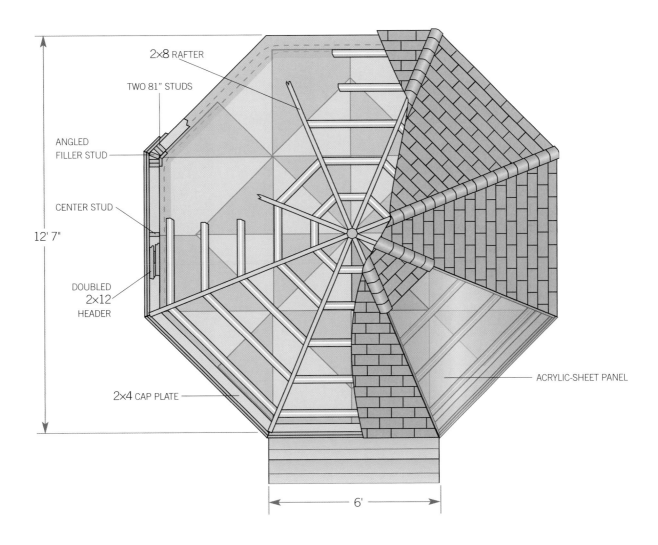

2×8 RAFTER

TWO 81" STUDS

ANGLED FILLER STUD

CENTER STUD

12' 7"

DOUBLED 2×12 HEADER

2×4 CAP PLATE

ACRYLIC-SHEET PANEL

6'

with the other wall sections. A dab of roofing cement or silicone sealant along the underside of the bottom plate will help hold it in position on the slab. Don't add the door-jamb stock yet.

5 **A substantial header** runs around the building to support the roof. To construct this header, fasten pairs of 6-foot-long 2-by-12 boards together, separated by 4-by-11¼-inch pieces of ½-inch exterior plywood. Place the plywood 2 inches from each end (to

clear the miter cuts to come), and on 2-foot centers in the middle; nail it in place with 8d nails. Measure and cut each header section to be flush with the outer edge of the cap plate, mitering the ends at 22½ degrees. Toenail the headers to the top plates and to each other with 16d nails. Top the headers with 2-by-4 cap plates, and nail them in place.

6 **To make the roof rafters,** take two 12-foot-long 2 by 8s and cut one end of each at a 45-degree

angle. Temporarily screw the cut ends to a scrap of 2 by 4 laid flat. Check that the rafters form a perfect 90-degree angle, and then add a temporary cross-brace made of plywood scrap about midway. With a helper, lift the assembly into position on the cap plate so the rafter ends bisect two opposite cap-plate corners. Center the assembly by measuring the overhang on each side, and then mark for the 1½-inch-deep bird's-mouth and 45-degree flush cuts at the tail of each rafter. Take the

FRAMING DETAIL
(TOP PLAN VIEW)

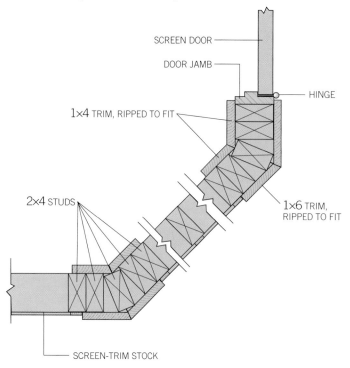

SCREEN DOOR

DOOR JAMB

HINGE

1×4 TRIM, RIPPED TO FIT

1×6 TRIM, RIPPED TO FIT

2×4 STUDS

SCREEN-TRIM STOCK

FOUNDATION DETAIL
(SIDE ELEVATION VIEW)

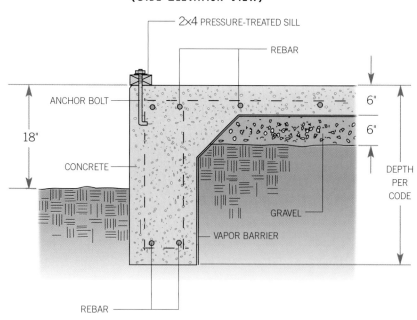

2×4 PRESSURE-TREATED SILL

REBAR

6"

6"

ANCHOR BOLT

18"

DEPTH PER CODE

CONCRETE

GRAVEL

VAPOR BARRIER

REBAR

assembly down, make the cuts, and then lift it back. Check the fit, and make adjustments as necessary. When you're satisfied with the fit, disassemble the rafters. Use the finished rafters to mark and cut six more.

7 **Rip the 4-foot-long** 4-by-4 king post on a table saw so that it has eight equal flats to accept the rafters and rafter braces. Attach a pair of rafters to opposite sides of the king post with metal framing connectors and proprietary screws. Measure and cut two rafter crossbraces, and attach them to the king post and rafters with metal framing connectors and screws. Be sure the crossbraces are level with each other and meet the king post at 90 degrees and the rafters at 45 degrees. Attach another set of rafters and braces to the king post, 90 degrees opposed to the first set. With helpers, lift this assembly into place and toenail it to the cap plate. Lift the remaining rafter pairs and braces into place and attach the rafters to the king post and cap plate.

8 **Cut and attach** the 2-by-4 roof purlins using metal framing connectors and proprietary screws. Measure, cut, and nail on ¾-inch plywood triangles atop the roof framing. If you're painting or staining the inner roof surface and framing, do it now. Add the clear acrylic-sheet section and its flashing, and seal it with silicone. With roofing nails, attach a metal drip edge to the roof perimeter (but not along the acrylic sheet). Shingle the roof (see pages 122–123). Bend and add hip shingles at the roof angles, and seal them with roofing cement. For the best appearance and weathertightness, top the roof with a custom-made metal cap, or with a cap made from cut shingles and roofing cement (the latter is more apt to leak).

9 **To cover the rough lumber** and rafter ends and create a finished appearance, measure, cut, and add 1-by-12 horizontal trim boards and 1-by-6 fascia to the roof header. Miter the corners at $22\frac{1}{2}$ degrees, and nail the boards to the header with 8d finish nails. With a table saw set for $22\frac{1}{2}$ degrees, rip 1-by-4 (inside) and 1-by-6 (outside) vertical trim boards for each corner; crosscut them to fit, and nail them on with 8d finish nails. Measure, cut, and nail jamb stock to the sides and top of the doorway, shimming as necessary to fit the doors. Cover the joint between the jambs and the framing with 1-by-4 and 1-by-6 trim, ripped to fit.

10 **Paint or stain** the structure and doors as desired, and hang the doors. Prepaint or stain the $\frac{3}{8}$-by-1-inch molding. Staple screening in place over the openings, crosscut the screen retainers to fit, and nail them on with 4d galvanized finish nails.

MATERIALS CHECKLIST

LUMBER

2x4 pressure-treated sills
2x4 framing
2x6 stair tread
2x8 rafters
2x12 headers (doubled) and stair stringers
4x4 king post
1x4, 1x6, and 1x12 trim
Door-jamb stock
$\frac{3}{8}$ x1-inch screen molding
$\frac{1}{2}$-inch exterior plywood spacers
$\frac{3}{4}$-inch exterior plywood

HARDWARE

$\frac{1}{2}$-inch anchor bolts, washers, and nuts
8d and 16d galvanized nails
4d and 8d galvanized finish nails
Galvanized roofing nails
Outdoor screws
Metal framing connectors and fasteners
Two 30-inch-by-7-foot screen doors; hinges and latches
Screening and staples

OTHER

Concrete, #3 and #5 rebar, and form lumber for foundation
Gravel
6-mil polyethylene vapor barrier
Silicone sealant
Roofing cement
Acrylic-sheet panel and metal flashing
Metal drip edge
Asphalt-fiberglass shingles
Custom-fabricated metal roof cap
Paint, stain, or wood preservative

building an open-air bedroom

"Back to nature" is the theme of this airy, detached sleeping hut. Simple enough to build in a weekend, it's easily scaled up or down and can be located nearly anywhere.

Ideal for alfresco sleeping, this hut could also function as a pool house, playhouse, or even a fair-weather office. George Bernard Shaw once had something like this. Containing only a chair, table, typewriter, and telephone, his hut sat on a pivot so it could turn to follow the sun in his garden (the phone, by the way, permitted only outgoing calls). If any of this sounds appealing, read on. It's hard to beat this design for maximum return on investment.

DESIGN DETAILS

True to its rustic roots, the hut emphasizes simple structure over style. The functional diagonal braces add a little rhythm to the facade, and the Victorian screen door provides a touch of whimsical charm. The floor is built like a house deck, providing ample drainage for wind-blown rain. If summers are stormy in your area, plan to extend the rafters and their supporting beams to enlarge the roof deck by a foot or so in each direction, which will provide a little more shelter. The roof deck is made of plywood, but tongue-and-groove boards line the underside for appearance' sake; alternatively, you could use rough-sawn or saw-kerfed plywood. Be sure that the metal drip edge you purchase will cover the full thickness of the roof deck. Note that the front of the hut is much higher than the back. In a mild climate, it's best to face the front to the south; in a hot climate, the hut will stay cooler if the front faces north.

BUILDING NOTES

As with most structures, the foundation and floor deck are built first; then the front and rear wall frames are erected. Because the face of the hut requires shear strength, the framing must be perfectly square, with good, tight joints. After the front and rear walls come the rafters, followed by the side-wall posts and braces, which must be built in place because they are fitted to the structure. The final steps are adding the roof, siding, screening, door, and trim.

Sleeping under the stars is bug-free in this simple screened structure.
Design: Jim Knott.

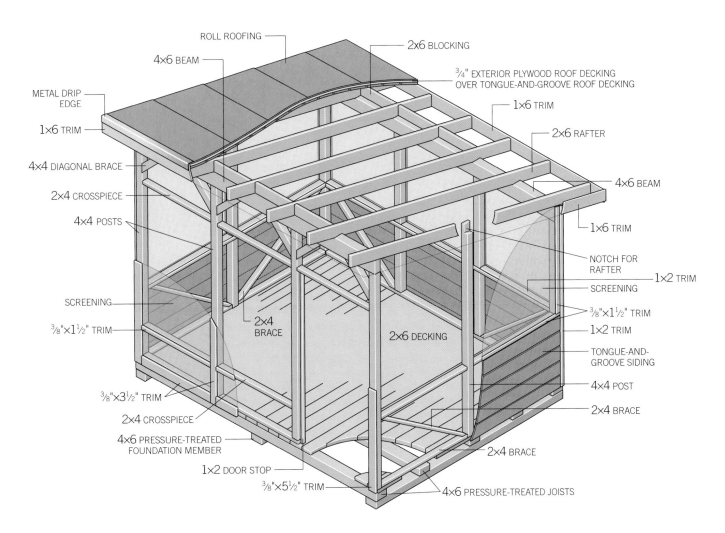

ROLL ROOFING

2x6 BLOCKING

4×6 BEAM

¾" EXTERIOR PLYWOOD ROOF DECKING
OVER TONGUE-AND-GROOVE ROOF DECKING

METAL DRIP
EDGE

1×6 TRIM

1×6 TRIM

2×6 RAFTER

4×4 DIAGONAL BRACE

4×6 BEAM

2×4 CROSSPIECE

1×6 TRIM

4×4 POSTS

NOTCH FOR
RAFTER

1×2 TRIM

SCREENING

SCREENING

⅜"×1½" TRIM

⅜"×1½" TRIM

2×4
BRACE

1×2 TRIM

2×6 DECKING

TONGUE-AND-
GROOVE SIDING

⅜"×3½" TRIM

4×4 POST

2×4 CROSSPIECE

2×4 BRACE

4×6 PRESSURE-TREATED
FOUNDATION MEMBER

1×2 DOOR STOP

2×4 BRACE

⅜"×5½" TRIM

4×6 PRESSURE-TREATED JOISTS

STEP-BY-STEP GUIDE

1 **Place, rake, and level** a 4-inch-deep gravel bed at least 10 by 12 feet in size. (This does not need to be dug in; in fact, placing it on undisturbed soil will provide for better drainage.) Lay three 8-foot-long pressure-treated 4-by-6 foundation members parallel to one another on the gravel. Space the outer ones so that the distance between their outer edges measures 10 feet; center the middle one between them. Level the tops, and make sure they are all at the same height. Put gravel against them to hold them in place. Check for square.

2 **Place five 10-foot-long** pressure-treated 4-by-6 joists across the foundation members, as shown. Place the edges of the outer joists flush with the ends of the foundation members; place the remaining three joists on 2-foot centers. Check for level and square, shimming low joists if necessary. Toe-nail the joists to the foundation members with 16d galvanized nails.

3 **Deck the platform** with 8-foot-long cedar or redwood 2 by 6s, fastening them with paired deck screws at each joist. If the boards are green, butt them together; if

they're dry, use a 16d nail as a spacer between them. If you live in an especially "buggy" area, you may want to staple screening across the foundation members before installing the decking.

4 **Build the front** and rear wall frames flat on the completed deck (don't raise them in place yet). The rear wall has a 10-foot-long 2-by-4 bottom plate nailed to the bases of four 6-foot-long 4-by-4 posts. The front wall has an 81½-inch bottom plate nailed to the three left-most 4-by-4 posts, which are each 94½ inches long.

The right-most post is 8 feet long; it will be fastened directly to the decking. Start by nailing the plates to the posts. Next, fasten 2-by-4 crosspieces and 4-by-4 diagonal braces in the locations shown, driving outdoor screws through angled pilot holes. Locate the middle crosspieces on the rear wall so that five 6-inch siding boards starting at the lower edge of the decking will overlap them by ¾ inch. Use 4d galvanized nails to fasten 1-by-2 trim to span the tops of the crosspieces and the posts on the inside. This enhances both appearance and strength. Don't add the beams across the tops of the walls until you've raised the walls.

5 **Fasten a temporary brace** across the doorway near the bottoms of the posts to hold the right-most post in place. With a helper, raise, plumb, and position the front wall. Screw its bottom plate to the decking with 3-inch outdoor screws, and temporarily brace the posts with diagonal 2 by 4s staked to the ground and tacked to the

MATERIALS CHECKLIST

LUMBER
4x6 pressure-treated foundation members and joists
4x6 beams
4x4 posts and braces
2x6 decking, rafters, and blocking
2x4 bottom plates, braces, and crosspieces
Cedar tongue-and-groove roof decking
¾-inch exterior plywood roof decking
6-inch cedar or redwood shiplap or tongue-and-groove siding
1x2 door stop and trim
⅜x5½-inch trim
⅜x3½-inch trim
⅜x1½-inch trim
1x6 trim

HARDWARE
4d, 8d, and 16d galvanized box nails
Galvanized roofing nails
3½-inch outdoor screws

OTHER
Gravel
Roofing cement
Roll roofing and metal drip edge
Screening and staples
Screen door, hinges, and latch
Paint, stain, or wood preservative

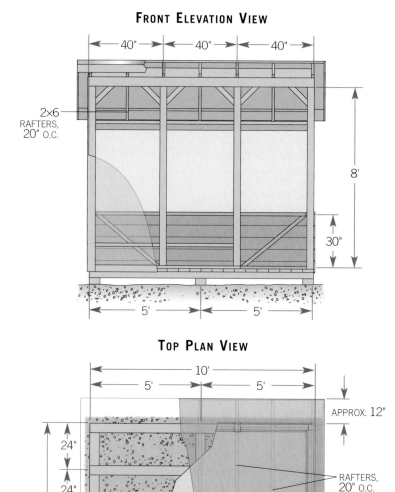

FRONT ELEVATION VIEW

2×6 RAFTERS, 20" O.C.

40" · 40" · 40"

8'

30"

5' · 5'

TOP PLAN VIEW

10'

5' · 5'

APPROX. 12"

24"

24"

8'

24"

24"

RAFTERS, 20" O.C.

APPROX. 6"

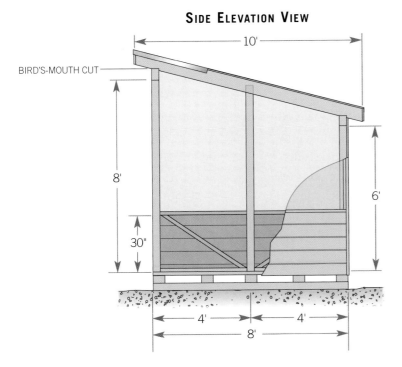

SIDE ELEVATION VIEW

BIRD'S-MOUTH CUT

10'

8'

30"

6'

4' 4'

8'

decking. Working from two ladders, set the 10-foot-long 4-by-6 beam across the tops of the posts, and fasten each post to the beam with four screws driven at an angle. Repeat this process with the back wall. Finally, cut the 1-foot-long 4-by-4 diagonal braces for the front wall so their ends are at 45-degree angles, and fasten them in place with screws.

6 **Take a 10-foot-long 2 by 6** and, with a helper, rest it on the front and back 4-by-6 beams. Square up the rafter, adjust it for equal overhangs at the front and rear, and then mark the rafter for the bird's-mouth cuts. Make the cuts, check the fit, adjust if necessary, and then use this rafter as a template for cutting the six others. Cut the remaining rafters, and fasten all of them in place, as

shown, driving pairs of screws at an angle at each connection. Cut 2-by-6 blocking to fit between the rafters atop the beams.

7 **Erect and plumb** the side posts in the center of each side wall. Notch them to interlock with the outer rafters, as shown. Fasten the tops and bottoms with outdoor screws. Measure, cut, and add the 2-by-4 braces at the top, diagonally, and across the bottom, fastening them with screws driven at an angle. Attach the 1-by-2 inside trim using 4d nails.

8 **Cut four pieces** of 1-by-2 trim to run vertically from the rafter edges to the bottom of the decking at the rear corners. Fasten the trim with 4d galvanized nails to the back corner posts. Cut and fasten the siding, butting the

boards against the corner trim pieces and nailing them with 4d nails. Let the side boards run long, then cut them flush with the front corner posts.

9 **Cut and nail** the tongue-and-groove roof decking to the rafters, best side down. Follow with a layer of ¾-inch plywood, nailing along the rafter locations. Next, add the metal drip edge, starting at the low end of the roof, working up the sides, and finishing at the high end. Cut the top and bottom pieces long enough to span the sides and go around the corners (cut the flashing just enough at the corners so you can bend it down). Finish the roof by nailing on the roll roofing, starting at the low end of the roof and working up. Trim the roofing to fit within the drip edge, and overlap pieces as recommended by the manufacturer. Use roofing cement to seal all seams and to fasten roll roofing to the drip edge.

10 **Before installing** screening, protect the wood with two coats of wood preservative, paint, or stain. Then staple the screening in place (see page 40) and cover the edges with prefinished ⅜-by-3½-inch and ⅜-by-1½-inch trim. Cover the front of the outer door post from the inner edge to the siding with a piece of prefinished ⅜-by-5½-inch trim. Fasten the 1-by-2 door stops with 4d nails, and hang the screen door (see page 74). Touch up any paint, stain, or preservative.

installing a screen door

As the portal between your yard and screened porch or patio, a screen door should allow easy passage for people but keep the bugs at bay.

Made with wood, vinyl, or aluminum frames, screen doors are available in a variety of styles at most home improvement centers. Though aluminum and vinyl are less expensive materials, wood is more solid and quieter, and it can be trimmed to fit. Sold in widths from 24 to 36 inches, screen doors are sized to fit standard door frames.

Though some screen doors are sold pre-hung in a door frame, it may be necessary to build your own frame made up of jambs and a threshold.

Build the door frame on a flat surface from ¾-inch-thick jamb stock, sized to fit around the screen door and with a ⅛-inch gap on all sides. The width of the jamb stock is determined by the overall thickness of the wall (wall studs plus any interior and/or exterior wall coverings). Glue and nail the side jambs to the head jamb and threshold using 10d galvanized nails.

Most vinyl and aluminum screen doors are sold with manufacturer's installation instructions, which should serve as your guide. The following tells how to install a wooden screen door.

Start by mounting the hinges on the jamb. Position a loose-pin butt-mortise hinge on the hinge-side jamb, about 7 inches down from the top, and outline it with a sharp utility knife. Then, using a wood chisel, cut a shallow mortise for the hinge so that it will sit flush with the jamb. Repeat this process for the lower hinge, about 11 inches up from the bottom. Screw the hinges in place, and then remove the hinge pins and the leaves that will attach to the door's edge.

Position the door frame in the rough opening so its edges are flush with the outer faces of the interior and exterior wall coverings. Drive pairs of tapered wooden shims (narrow shingles) between the jambs and the trimmer studs to adjust the unit, and hold it in place until you nail it.

Fasten the lower hinge side of the door first. Position the nail where the stop molding will cover it, and then nail through the jamb and shims partway (about 1 inch) and into the stud with a 16d finish nail. Make sure the jamb is plumb, adjust with shims if necessary, and fasten the upper hinge side of the door using the same method. Repeat along the center and then along the latch edge of the jamb. Caulk along the base of the threshold.

Stand the door in the frame to check its fit. If it must be trimmed slightly, it's generally best to trim off the hinge-side edge of the door rather than the latch-side

A screen door can be as fashionable as it is functional, lending an element of style to your screened room.

ROUGH FRAMING

2×4 CRIPPLE STUD

DOUBLED 2×4 HEADER

2×4 KING STUD

2×4 KING STUD

2×4 TRIMMER STUDS

RAILING

DECK

BOTTOM PLATE

JAMB ASSEMBLY

DOUBLED 2×4 HEADER

³⁄₄"-THICK JAMB STOCK

MORTISE FOR HINGE

SHIMS

SCREENING

HINGE

DOOR STOP

1×4 OR 1×6 TRIM

THRESHOLD

PNEUMATIC DOOR CLOSER

JAMB-MOUNTING BRACKET

HINGE JAMB

SCREEN-DOOR FRAME

DOOR STOP

DOOR-MOUNTING BRACKET

edge so you don't cause problems with the fit of the latch.

Stain or paint the screen door with an exterior finish before hanging it, and then touch it up afterward. Be sure to seal the door's top and bottom edges with the finish to prevent moisture from infiltrating and swelling or rotting the wood.

Shim the door in the frame with $\frac{1}{8}$-inch tolerances at the top, bottom, and sides. Use a sharp pencil to precisely mark the positions of the hinge leaves on the door's edge. Remove the door, and finish marking the hinge leaves' positions on the edge of the door, guiding your pencil with a combination square. Use a sharp

utility knife to score deeply along the cutting lines, and then use a chisel to cut shallow mortises so the hinge leaves will sit flush.

Attach the hinge leaves to the door's edge with $1\frac{1}{2}$-inch screws. Re-couple the door's hinge leaves with the jamb's, and slide the hinge pins into place. Be sure the door swings and closes properly and maintains a $\frac{1}{8}$-inch gap around its perimeter. Then screw on the screen door's handle.

After hanging the screen door, use 6d galvanized finish nails to attach door-stop molding around the inner perimeter of the jambs where it will keep the outer face of the screen door flush with the outer edges of the jambs. Trim off

the shims, and cover the gap between the jamb and the wall frame with casing.

You may want to add a couple of amenities that will improve your screen door's performance. A pneumatic door closer will keep the door from slamming, and a flexible sweep attached to the bottom edge of the door will keep out insects and dirt. Install these according to the product manufacturers' directions.

creating a three-season room

Screened-room owners love their screened rooms. In fact, most will tell you they wish their screened room could be used year-round.

Heatable, insulated screen rooms that can be buttoned up with windows may remain usable during cold, wintry weather, but what about the rest? How do you extend the usable period of a screened room to take advantage of those fair winter days when the sun is low in the sky? By blocking the breezes and capturing the radiant heat.

To do this, you can install glass or acrylic covers over screened openings. Here we offer three variations to consider: storm windows, permanent doors and windows, and a unique solution that quickly provides windows when you need them and removes them when you don't.

FLIP-UP WINDOWS

Intended for a summer cabin in an area subject to sudden summer storms, the clever flip-up windows shown here are great for quickly sealing off—or ventilating—a screened room at any time of the year. Going up and going down, their action is easy, fast, and smooth. Fixed glass panels at floor level expand the open feel of the walls from the interior.

This project won't work as a retrofit on just any given porch or screened room. The entire

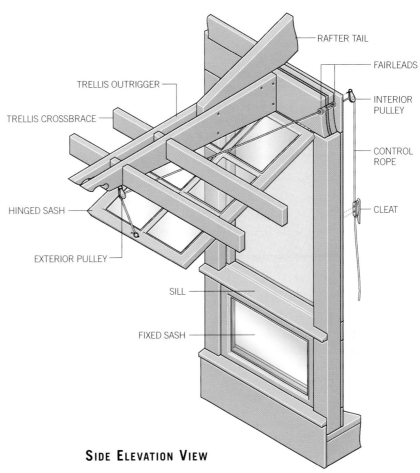

FLIP-UP-WINDOW CONSTRUCTION

RAFTER TAIL

FAIRLEADS

TRELLIS OUTRIGGER

INTERIOR PULLEY

TRELLIS CROSSBRACE

CONTROL ROPE

HINGED SASH

CLEAT

EXTERIOR PULLEY

SILL

FIXED SASH

structure was designed by an architect and built as new construction. The window bays are sized to fit available window sashes; an exterior trellis structure was built onto the eaves of the room to support the sashes in the open position. Plenty of clearance was provided around the room's perimeter so that, when the windows are pulled into their open position, they don't become a head-bumping hazard.

A simple rope-and-pulley system raises and lowers the window sashes, which are hinged along their tops. A separate cord pulls them tight, but you could omit the cord in favor of standard window latches.

For best results, visit a marine hardware store to purchase the pulley system. Look for synthetic yacht braid (⅜-inch braid is about right); small pulleys called blocks; tubular fairleads; and plastic or metal jam cleats, which make it easy to tie off the ropes quickly.

This screened room was designed with enough space around its perimeter to accommodate a system of operable window sashes, which allows for year-round comfort. Design: M. Taylor Dawson III/ Wilson & Dawson Architects

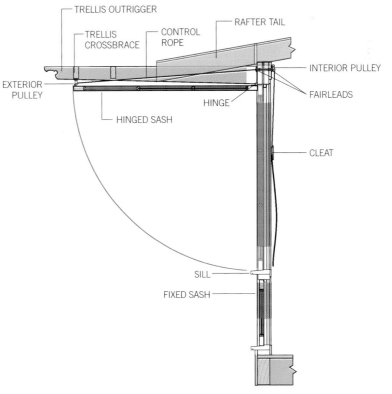

SIDE ELEVATION VIEW

TRELLIS OUTRIGGER

RAFTER TAIL

TRELLIS CROSSBRACE

CONTROL ROPE

INTERIOR PULLEY

EXTERIOR PULLEY

FAIRLEADS

HINGE

HINGED SASH

CLEAT

SILL

FIXED SASH

Sliding doors and screens allow this room to serve as an indoor/outdoor space.

MOVABLE DOORS AND WINDOWS

Another way to capture warmth is to install (or retrofit) windows in the bays that might otherwise be simple screened openings. The photograph above shows wood-framed glass doors that slide to cover screen doors. The generously sized openings allow ample breezes to blow through in the summer but are quickly and easily closed off when the winds howl. Tall fixed windows flank the doors to let in more light. Though it does not provide as much ventilation as a screened room, this option does create a well-sealed four-season room.

INSTALLING STORM WINDOWS

Storm windows are the most obvious solution for blocking winter breezes and capturing radiant warmth. They also will reduce the fading of furnishings in the winter months, when the low-angle sun can be especially damaging.

You can buy stock sizes of storm windows or make your own. The easiest do-it-yourself products are sash kits designed to work with clear acrylic sheets, available at home improvement centers. The resulting windows can fit over your screened openings either outside or inside.

Commercial storm windows

will have their own proprietary hardware, which is usually easy to adapt to screened bays.

The illustrations on the facing page provide one example of a home-built storm sash, a design that's easy to mount over the screened openings typical of this book's projects. Build the inner frame first. Using a table saw or router, cut a rabbet groove along one edge of each frame's 1 by 2s to receive the acrylic panel. Miter the corners, and glue and screw them together. Then build the outer frame to fit around the inner one. Use flat metal L-shaped brackets to reinforce the corners. Screw the inner and outer frames together. Fasten the acrylic sheet in place with pieces of ¼-inch quarter-round molding.

Seal the homemade storm windows over their openings with foam, V-type, or tube-type weatherstripping, and secure the storm's sash to the surrounding framing or molding with half-turn buttons.

Some prefabricated storm windows come with their own screen units. You can kill two birds with one stone—providing both screens and windows—if you choose these. Then again, this method tends to work only if you're building a screened room from scratch; stock sizes are unlikely to fit an existing room's openings.

Before choosing glass for storm windows, consider weight. Glass storm windows may be quite heavy—and cumbersome to store. It's best to choose glass for openings no wider than 42 inches.

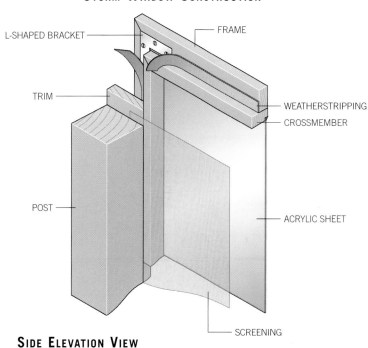

STORM-WINDOW CONSTRUCTION

L-SHAPED BRACKET
FRAME
TRIM
WEATHERSTRIPPING
CROSSMEMBER
POST
ACRYLIC SHEET
SCREENING

SIDE ELEVATION VIEW

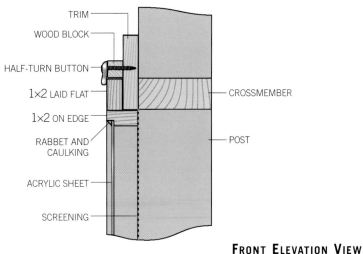

TRIM
WOOD BLOCK
HALF-TURN BUTTON
1×2 LAID FLAT
1×2 ON EDGE
RABBET AND CAULKING
ACRYLIC SHEET
SCREENING
CROSSMEMBER
POST

FRONT ELEVATION VIEW

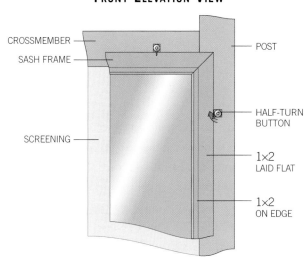

CROSSMEMBER
SASH FRAME
SCREENING
POST
HALF-TURN BUTTON
1×2 LAID FLAT
1×2 ON EDGE

Storm windows, particularly if made from lightweight acrylic and attached with clips, can be removed and stored in a snap.

The right mix of natural light, ventilation, and air flow will make your screened space more comfortable.

improving light and comfort

Skylights, ceiling fans, shutters, and similar amenities can help you increase or control light and ventilation in a screened room, extending the hours—and seasons—that the space can be enjoyed.

Because a screened room does not fully qualify as being either an indoor or an outdoor room, it has a climate all its own. Many screened rooms are built with minimal insulation, so they heat up quickly on sunny days.

And, because many screening fabrics admit heat but slow down breezes and reduce natural light, screened rooms can be somewhat dim and, at times, stuffy spaces.

Fortunately, these two common problems are easily remedied. To handle the problem of diminished light levels, you can install one or more skylights. In fact, by installing an operable skylight, you can solve two problems—you will flood the space with natural light while providing an escape route for heat. Alternatively, you can utilize translucent roof panels to increase natural light. To further stir up breezes, boosting comfort on hot, still days, you can install a ceiling fan.

Right: A screened-room addition could block natural light and darken adjacent spaces. In this house, tall open bays let plenty of light shine right through the addition and into the house.
Below: Louvered screens are great for controlling the amount of light and heat that enters a space—and can be easily adjusted over the course of the day.

Left: Translucent roof panels act as an oversized skylight, making the corner of this screened room as bright as the outdoors. *Above:* Tall screened windows flank this door. When open, they welcome breezes without allowing pests in or pets out.

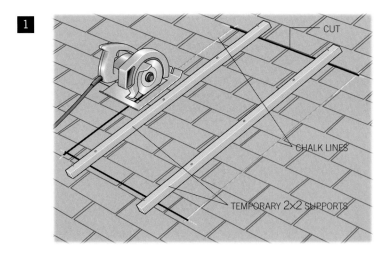

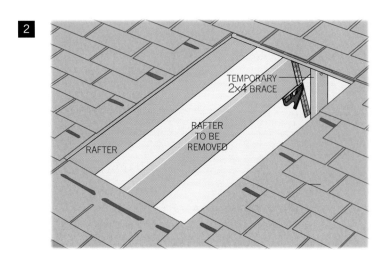

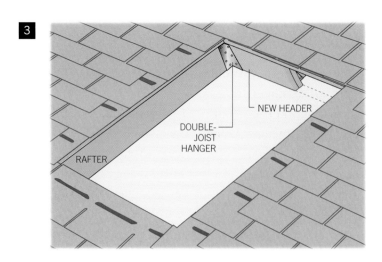

INSTALLING A SKYLIGHT

Skylights, available in various shapes and sizes, can be purchased as prefabricated kits that include the window (or "light"), which is usually made of acrylic or tempered glass, attached to a flanged frame that's made to be nailed onto the roof.

Following are the steps for installing a skylight into an existing roof with a cathedral-style ceiling (where beams and rafters are exposed), a situation typical of many screened rooms. Installing a skylight in a new roof is a similar, even easier job.

To simplify your work, choose a skylight that will fit between the room's ceiling beams or rafters or require removal of only one rafter. Be sure to choose the skylight's location carefully—the direct sun on a west- or south-facing skylight can quickly overwhelm its ventilation purpose. Also avoid placing it where there are any obstructions, such as wiring.

1 **Mark where the corners** of the skylight will be on the ceiling, and drive nails up through the roof at these spots. Then, on the roof, snap chalk lines between the marker nails to create the outline of the skylight. Cut the shingles along these lines, using a circular saw with an old carbide-tipped blade. Be sure to adjust the blade's depth so it will cut through the roofing material and sheathing but not into the rafters.

To prevent the cutout from dropping, temporarily nail a pair of 2 by 2s across the top, as shown, before you finish the cuts.

Carefully remove the shingles around the opening (you'll need some of them for replacement purposes), and pry up the sheathing. Peel back or remove the shingles at the top and sides to allow for the skylight's flange.

2 **To remove a rafter** (if necessary), determine the location and angle of the cuts. When doing this, allow for 3-inch headers that will span the top and bottom of the opening. Before cutting the rafter, support it above and below the cutout by temporarily nailing vertical 2-by-4 braces to the rafter. Mark the cutting lines with a square or adjustable T-bevel, and then cut through the rafters. If you're unsure how to do this, consult a professional.

3 **Measure and cut** headers, made of paired 2-bys that are the same width as the rafters. Before installing each header, pair up its two pieces and nail them together, staggering nails 6 inches apart along the length and driving two nails in at each end. Mount each header to the rafters with double-joist hangers or, if it will sit at an angle to the rafter, with framing anchors. Toenail (or mount with joist hangers) the cut-off rafter ends to the headers. Once you've secured the headers, remove the temporary braces.

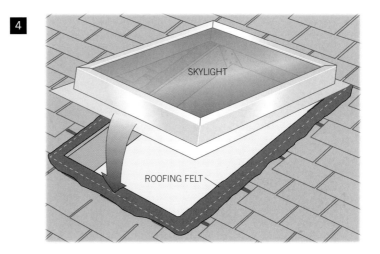

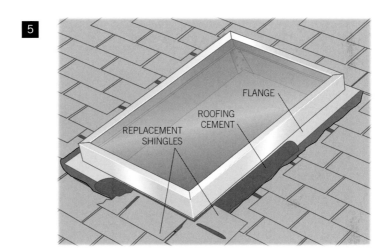

4 **To set the skylight,** cover the sheathing around the opening with roofing felt. If necessary, slide pieces under the existing felt above the cutout, and trim them at the edges of the opening. Using a putty knife, apply roofing cement in a swath 4 inches wide and ¼ inch thick around the opening. Set the skylight down over the hole, and press the metal flange firmly into the band of roofing cement. At the top and sides, slip the flange beneath the roofing shingles. At the bottom, allow the flange to rest on top of the shingles.

5 **Follow the directions** provided by the manufacturer for fastening the flange to the sheathing. Apply more roofing cement over the flange, covering the screws or nails. Press a shingle into the cement along the bottom of the skylight. Then replace the shingles at the sides and top, shingling right up to the sides of the skylight.

INSTALLING A CEILING FAN

One of the best ways to keep a screened room cool despite hot outdoor temperatures and reduced air flow is to install a ceiling fan. Choose one that will survive the moist conditions of a screened room. It should be "damp-rated" or, if it will be exposed to corrosive coastal air or particularly moist conditions, "wet-rated."

If you are installing a fan in a location where a light fixture already exists, the transformation is relatively easy because the wiring is in place for both the fan and a switch. (You can buy a fan that includes a light, so you won't have to sacrifice illumination).

Of course, there may not be a light conveniently located right where you want to put a fan. In this case, an electrician must install an electrical fixture box for the ceiling fan and run an electrical circuit to the box. Exactly how this is done depends on the situation. If the area has an attic, wires may be run through that space. On an exposed-beam ceiling, surface conduit may have to be run inconspicuously to a surface-mounted electrical box.

If the wiring for a switch isn't already in place, you can simplify the installation by installing a fan that is controlled by a pull chain or by a remote.

High ceilings are optimum for fan placement—in fact, a ceiling 8 feet or higher is mandatory, as most fans tend to hang down a foot or so. You can use downrod extensions, available in various lengths, to lower the fan's height (if the ceiling is particularly high) or to distance the blades from an angled ceiling.

Determine the fan's size by examining the room's size. The chart at bottom left offers guidelines to help in your selection.

Although you should follow the manufacturer's instructions, the following steps will give you a basic understanding of how most ceiling fans are installed. If you're unsure about any of the work involved, consult an electrician.

When replacing an existing light fixture, you'll need to remove the existing electrical box and install a special box made for hanging a ceiling fan. *Before you begin, turn off the electrical power to the circuit that serves the light at the electrical panel.*

Disassemble the light fixture, and unscrew it from the ceiling box. Then loosen or bend back the cable clamps that secure the electrical cable inside the box. Use a hammer and a short wooden block to dislodge the box from the

A ceiling fan increases ventilation in this decktop screened room. A high ceiling such as this is ideal for safe fan placement.

FAN-SIZE GUIDELINES

ROOM SIZE	FAN DIAMETER
Up to 64 square feet	36 inches
Up to 144 square feet	42 inches
Up to 225 square feet	44 inches
Up to 400 square feet	52 inches

ceiling framing. Pull the cable free from the box, and, if it's difficult to remove the box through the ceiling hole, leave the box in the ceiling cavity. Then install the fan.

1 First, install a fan brace. You can attach a brace between joists, using screws, if you have access from the attic. Otherwise, use a retrofit fan brace. This special shaft, designed to slip through the ceiling hole and then expand to wedge solidly between ceiling joists, provides the type of support required by a ceiling fan. Slip it through the hole, rest its feet on the backside of the ceiling, and rotate the shaft to secure it firmly. Center the U-shaped metal saddle over the hole, and snap it onto the brace. Thread the electrical wires through the cable clamp on the new metal fan box.

2 Screw the box to the saddle on the fan brace. Secure the bare grounding wire to the green grounding screw.

3 Screw the hanger bracket onto the box using the special screws provided. If the ceiling angles upward, the open side of the bracket should face the high side.

4 Assemble the fan's motor unit and downrod, and then fasten and tighten the downrod in its collar. Slide the collar, canopy, and ball onto the downrod, running the wires out the top of the ball. A pin that passes horizontally through

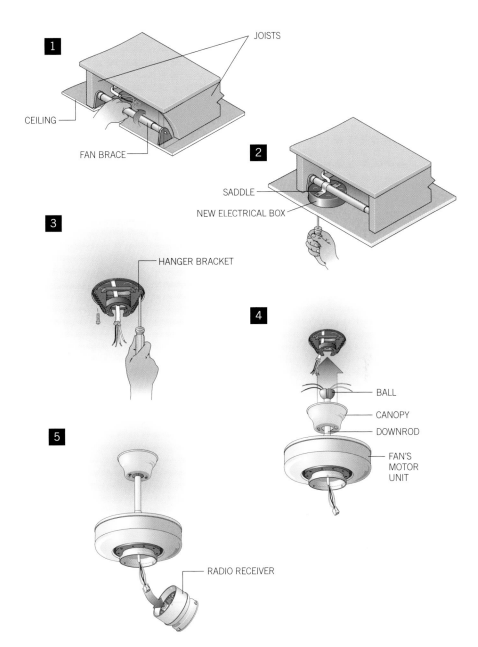

the top of the downrod holds the ball in place; after pushing this through the holes in the downrod, pull the ball up over the pin and secure it with its set screw. Lift the assembly up, and slide the ball into the hanger bracket. Rotate it until the ball locks.

5 Twist and connect the wires with wire nuts, according to the directions. In most cases, you'll be

connecting the fan's green wire to the box's bare (grounding) wire, the fan's white wire to the box's white (neutral) wire, and the fan motor's black and blue wires to the box's black (hot) wire. Carefully push the connected wires up into the box and screw the canopy in place. Last, add the radio receiver to the bottom of the fan for the remote control, and secure the fan blades to the motor unit.

Quality materials, sound building practices, and a simple design were all that was needed to transform this patio into a classic screened room.

building techniques

IF YOU'RE READY TO ROLL UP YOUR SLEEVES AND STRAP ON A TOOL BELT,

you've come to the right place. Creating a screened enclosure can be

as simple as mounting window screens in a porch's framework or as

complex as building an entire screened-in structure from scratch. This

chapter details the step-by-step techniques used to build screened

enclosures; many of these procedures are used in most of the projects

shown on pages 38–85. ■ The chapter begins with a look at the most

common materials used for building screened rooms, including lumber,

fasteners, and other hardware. From there, it moves through the various

stages of building screened-room structures, from casting a foundation

to constructing a roof. ■ Whether you're planning on designing your own

structure or modifying one of this book's designs, it's a good idea to read

through the entire chapter so you will have

a clear understanding of the construction

techniques involved. As a basic build-

ing reference, it will help you think

through your project's assembly be-

fore finalizing your design.

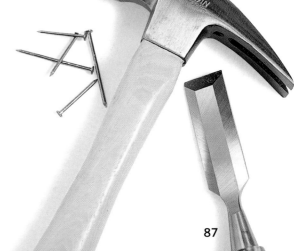

buying materials

The following primer can help you get through the lumberyard or home improvement center with a minimum of confusion and expense.

Building a screened enclosure typically involves working with a variety of materials, from lumber to screening. Here is a closer look at the right materials to buy.

LUMBER

Softwood lumber, the most common outdoor building material, varies by grade, species, type, size, and finish. Following are a few basics to advise your purchase.

GRADES When lumber is milled, it is sorted and then identified with a stamp indicating quality, moisture content, grade, and, in many cases, species and the grading agency (for example, "WWP" stands for the Western Wood Products Association).

Grading methods vary by species, but, in general, lumber grades depend on natural growth characteristics such as knots, defects resulting from milling errors, and manufacturing techniques used for drying and preserving the wood. These factors affect each piece's strength, durability, and appearance.

In most cases, you get what you pay for. The fewer the knots and other defects, the pricier the board. An excellent way to save money on a project is to pinpoint the least expensive grades suitable for the project's various components according to their strength and visibility requirements.

SPECIES Woods from different trees have different properties of

strength, workability, and durability. Most notable for their use in outdoor projects are redwood and cedar heartwoods (the darker part of the wood cut from the tree's core), which have a natural resistance to decay. This quality, combined with their natural beauty, makes redwood and cedar favored for applications that are exposed to the elements. These woods tend to be more expensive than ordinary structural woods such as Douglas fir, yellow southern pine, and western larch, so, where paint or stain will cover or where components will be hidden, many landscape professionals specify Douglas fir and ensure durability with a protective finish (see page 106 for more about finishing).

TREATED LUMBER Lumber that has been pressure treated with preservatives at the factory can survive outdoors for decades longer than untreated wood. This lumber costs more and may have to be specially ordered, but it is less likely to split or crack. Foundation grade should be used for any wood that contacts the ground. The American Wood Preserver's Bureau, which gov-

WESTERN RED CEDAR

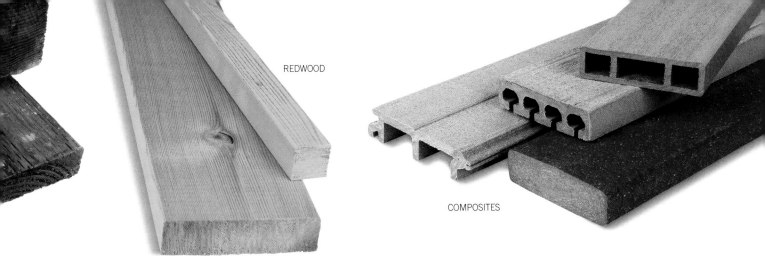

REDWOOD

COMPOSITES

erns this industry, grade-stamps preservative-treated lumber; look for its stamp. For information on the safe handling of pressure-treated lumber, see page 112.

SURFACE FINISH Most lumberyards handle both rough and surfaced lumber. Rough lumber is available only in the lower grades, which have more defects and higher moisture content. Surfaced lumber, the standard for most construction, comes in nearly all grades. If you like a rustic look but want a quality grade of wood, you can special-order resawn lumber.

STANDARD SIZES Lumber is normally stocked in lengths of 6 to 20 feet and in a broad range of widths and thicknesses. When you work with standard surfaced lumber, be aware that a finished 2 by 4 is not 2 inches by 4 inches. The nominal size of lumber is designated before the piece is dried and surfaced, so the actual finished size is always less. For the actual sizes of nominal dimensions, see the chart at right.

When calculating the sizes of lumber needed to support loads, use the chart on page 98 as a guide. The dimensions given are minimums—larger beams and joists can span greater distances between posts or supports. Select larger sizes where you need to carry excessive loads or where appearance matters. Be aware that your area's building codes may vary from the standards given here; always defer to local codes.

COMPOSITE LUMBER

Products made from recycled plastic and wood chips and solid vinyl are rapidly gaining popularity as outdoor building materials—particularly for decking, railings, and other elements that are heavily exposed to weather—because they are impervious to decay. Decking planks are solid, tongue-and-groove, or web-like in construction, and they come in a variety of colors. Some composites are intended to mimic the look of real wood, while others make no such attempt. Composites will not splinter or crack like wood and require little maintenance beyond periodic cleaning. They usually can be cut, drilled, installed, and painted or stained like solid wood. Most composites are not suitable for structural members.

STANDARD DIMENSIONS OF SOFTWOODS

NOMINAL	ACTUAL
1 x 2	$\frac{3}{4}$" x $1\frac{1}{2}$"
1 x 3	$\frac{3}{4}$" x $2\frac{1}{2}$"
1 x 4	$\frac{3}{4}$" x $3\frac{1}{2}$"
1 x 6	$\frac{3}{4}$" x $5\frac{1}{2}$"
1 x 8	$\frac{3}{4}$" x $7\frac{1}{4}$"
1 x 10	$\frac{3}{4}$" x $9\frac{1}{4}$"
1 x 12	$\frac{3}{4}$" x $11\frac{1}{4}$"
2 x 2	$1\frac{1}{2}$" x $1\frac{1}{2}$"
2 x 3	$1\frac{1}{2}$" x $2\frac{1}{2}$"
2 x 4	$1\frac{1}{2}$" x $3\frac{1}{2}$"
2 x 6	$1\frac{1}{2}$" x $5\frac{1}{2}$"
2 x 8	$1\frac{1}{2}$" x $7\frac{1}{4}$"
2 x 10	$1\frac{1}{2}$" x $9\frac{1}{4}$"
2 x 12	$1\frac{1}{2}$" x $11\frac{1}{4}$"
4 x 4	$3\frac{1}{2}$" x $3\frac{1}{2}$"
4 x 6	$3\frac{1}{2}$" x $5\frac{1}{2}$"
4 x 8	$3\frac{1}{2}$" x $7\frac{1}{4}$"
4 x 10	$3\frac{1}{2}$" x $9\frac{1}{4}$"
6 x 8	$5\frac{1}{2}$" x $7\frac{1}{4}$"

PLYWOOD AND STRUCTURAL WOOD PANELS

For gazebos or similar outdoor structures, exterior plywood is often used for roof or wall sheathing and as form-making material for casting concrete.

The front and back surfaces of standard plywood are graded for quality. Letters A through D designate the grades, A being the highest. A/C (exterior) panels are good choices where only one side will be visible. Face and back grades and interior or exterior designations should be stamped on the back or edge of each panel along with an association trademark that assures quality (such as "APA," which stands for the Engineered Wood Association).

Before installing plywood, seal all edges with a water repellent, stain sealer, or exterior-house-paint primer. Restain or repaint the panels' surfaces every five years to maintain protection.

SCREENING

Aluminum and vinyl-coated fiberglass are by far the most common screening fabrics used to enclose screened rooms. Of the two, vinyl-coated fiberglass is more popular because it's about half the price of aluminum.

Screening is created by weaving metal wire or spun-glass filaments with a vinyl coating on a modified loom. The typical size of an individual wire or filament for window screening is .011 mil (inch); heavy-duty varieties for pool enclosures, patio rooms, and some screen doors utilize .013-mil (inch) strands.

The density of the mesh determines its strength, the size of the bugs it will hold at bay, and the amount of light and breezes it will permit. The most common mesh size is called an "18 by 16," which designates that there are 18 horizontal and 16 vertical strands per square inch. Because 18-by-14 mesh usually uses larger strands, it's typically chosen for pool enclosures, porches, and the like. If you want to stop tiny bugs such as no-see-ums, you can buy 20-by-20 mesh, but this will cut down on light transmission and breezes.

Do-it-yourself varieties of screening are sold at hardware stores and home centers. Rolls are 7 or 25 feet long and come 24, 28, 30, 32, 36, and 48 inches wide. Longer 100-foot rolls are also available in other widths, including 18, 20, 22, 26, 34, 42, 54, 70, 72, and 84 inches.

Alternatively, you can buy screens through a screen shop and have them installed professionally. To find a dealer, simply look up "Screens—Door & Window" in the Yellow Pages.

METAL SCREENING Aluminum is relatively strong, durable, and, at 30 to 35 cents per square foot, moderately priced. Typical finishes are black, dark gray, and silver gray with a clear coating to protect the sheen. (Darker colors reflect less light, making them easier to look through from inside.)

TYPES OF SCREENING FABRICS

VINYL-COATED FIBERGLASS ALUMINUM SOLAR

Bronze screening is similar to aluminum but is far more expensive. Even more high-end are fabrics made of copper, brass, or stainless steel. All of these, except brass, are typically made from a .011-mil wire size in an 18-by-14 or 16-by-16 mesh. Brass is made with heavier wire: .018 mil in a 16-by-16 mesh.

Bronze is the least expensive, at about $1 per square foot. Copper and stainless steel are closer to $1.20 per square foot. Brass, at about $2.15 per square foot, is the most expensive.

When new, bronze has a golden shine. Copper, bronze, and brass will eventually take on a verdigris patina. Stainless steel, the strongest, stays a shiny silver. Copper, bronze, and brass should

not be installed in aluminum screen frames because the different metals will corrode where they come in contact.

VINYL-COATED FIBERGLASS
SCREENING
Vinyl-coated fiberglass doesn't corrode, rust, or stain, but it can stretch out of shape and tear more easily than aluminum. Vinyl-coated fiberglass screening is available in dark gray, silver gray, and aquamarine.

Solar or "sun" screening is a tightly woven, energy-efficient variation of vinyl-coated fiberglass that is used for window and door screening and patio, porch, and pool enclosures. It provides excellent shading, protecting against heat gain and fading caused by sunlight. On the downside, you

will give up about 30 percent of light transmission. During the daytime, it appears almost opaque from outside but offers good visibility from inside. Available colors include charcoal, bronze, dark bronze, silver gray, and gold (charcoal and silver gray are the most common). Rolls of sun screening run 30 by 60 inches, 36 by 60 inches, 36 by 84 inches, and 48 by 84 inches. In addition, you can buy 100-foot-long rolls in various widths. Prices typically range from 15 to 25 cents per square foot.

SPECIALTY SCREENING
If you have a cat or dog that is inclined to scratch or shred screens, consider pet-screen fabric made from heavy-duty, vinyl-coated polyester, sold in black or gray.

For replacing patio-door screens, you can buy a flexible, nylon-reinforced material that will stretch without sagging. A kit for one door sells for between $20 and $24.

To temporarily screen a garage, boathouse, porch, or similar large structure during bug season, you can buy a special garage-door screen kit. With this system, you circle the opening with a special tape or strip that grabs onto the vinyl-coated fiberglass screening. A breeze to install, it fits openings that are 7 by 9 or 7 by 16 feet; custom sizes are also available. Kits run from $80 to $100. (If you have two or three smaller openings, you can chop

BRONZE   PET-RESISTANT   20-BY-20 MESH

up one or two kits to handle the various sizes.)

Screen Tight™ is an alternative to conventional methods used for screening porches. A patented spline system makes installing and repairing the screening relatively easy. First, vinyl bases are fastened to the porch structure. Then, vinyl splines lock the screening to the base, and a cap covers the connection. Including screening material, this system runs about $1 per square foot of opening; the average cost per porch is $180.

You can also buy retractable screens for both windows and doors. The entire screen rolls back into a tubular casing at one side of the opening when not in use. When open, the screen is held in place by magnetic catches. Several colors are available. Including installation, prices run from $285 for a single door to $595 for double doors (windows are custom priced).

NAIL EQUIVALENTS

PENNY	ACTUAL
2d	1"
4d	1½"
6d	2"
8d	2½"
10d	3"
12d	3¼"
16d	3½"
20d	4"

NAILS AND SCREWS

Nails are sold in 1-, 5-, and 50-pound boxes or loose in bins. "Penny" (abbreviated "d" from the Latin *denarius*) indicates a nail's length. The chart below gives measurements in inches for the most common sizes.

Use hot-dipped galvanized, aluminum, or stainless-steel nails outdoors—other types will rust. In fact, even the best hot-dipped nail may rust over time, particularly at the exposed nailhead, where the coating is usually battered by a hammer. Stainless-steel or aluminum nails won't rust, but they cost several times as much as galvanized nails. In many cases, they must be specially ordered.

The common nail, which has an extra-thick shank and a broad head, is favored for construction because it is easiest to drive without it bending. If you don't want a nailhead to show, choose a finishing nail, which has a small, slightly rounded head. After you drive it nearly flush, use a nail set to sink the head just below the surface of the wood.

Though more expensive than nails, coated or galvanized outdoor screws offer several advantages. They drive easily into redwood and cedar, their coating is less likely to be damaged during installation, and they are easier to remove when repairs are required. However, they are not rated for shear strength, so opt for nails, lag screws, or bolts for heavy-duty situations.

LAG SCREWS AND BOLTS

Bolts and lag screws are recommended for any connection where strength is particularly important (beam-to-post, ledger-to-house, and so forth).

Typical lengths range from 3 to 12 inches, and diameters range from ¼ to ¾ inch in $\frac{1}{16}$-inch increments. A bolt should be approximately 1 inch longer than the combined thickness of the pieces being joined to accommodate washers and a nut. Predrill a bolt

NAILS, SCREWS, AND BOLTS

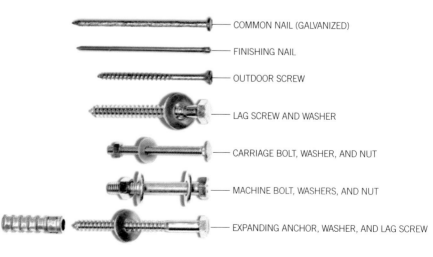

— COMMON NAIL (GALVANIZED)

— FINISHING NAIL

— OUTDOOR SCREW

— LAG SCREW AND WASHER

— CARRIAGE BOLT, WASHER, AND NUT

— MACHINE BOLT, WASHERS, AND NUT

— EXPANDING ANCHOR, WASHER, AND LAG SCREW

FRAMING CONNECTORS

BOLT-DOWN POST BASE

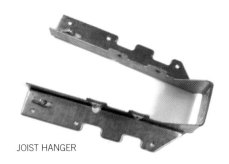

JOIST HANGER

EMBEDDED POST BASE

POST CAP

connectors—including joist hangers, post bases, and post caps—in sizes that will fit most standard-dimension rough and surfaced lumber. Choose connectors that are electroplated or hot-dipped galvanized to avoid rust. If you can't find appropriate connectors, a welder can fabricate decorative or specialty supports.

When using framing connectors, be sure to use the sizes and the types of nails or fasteners specified by the manufacturer.

hole using a drill bit of the same diameter as the bolt's shank. Place a washer under the nut and under the head of a machine bolt (don't place one under a carriage-bolt head because it's designed to bite into the wood so the bolt won't turn as you tighten the nut).

Lag screws (sometimes called lag bolts) come in equivalent sizes and can substitute for bolts in certain situations. They are particularly useful in tight spots where you can reach only one side of the connection with a wrench (a socket wrench is the easiest to use). Predrill a lead hole about two-thirds the length of the lag screw using a drill bit ⅛-inch diameter smaller than the lag screw's shank. Place a washer under the head of the lag screw before driving in the screw.

It's better to form a connection

with many small-diameter bolts or lag screws rather than with a few large-diameter bolts. The right number and sizes will depend on the width of the lumber that is being joined.

If you need to secure a ledger to a masonry wall, anchor posts to a slab floor, or similarly fasten material to concrete, use expanding anchors. These have an expanding collar or prongs that grip the surrounding hole firmly when a lag screw is driven home.

FRAMING CONNECTORS

Metal connectors make joining structural framing materials an easier job and strengthen joints. They are used throughout this book's projects but are often hidden from view.

Most lumberyards and home centers stock a variety of framing

ESTIMATING AND ORDERING MATERIALS

Before you even think about putting together a materials list, make sure you have a workable set of plans. Carefully think through the building process, and then count up the pieces you'll need. Specify lumber sizes, grades, and surface finishes. Do the same for the other materials.

To reduce the cost of materials, order as much as possible at a single time from a single supplier. Choose your supplier on the basis of competitive bids from several retailers, and order materials in regularly available, standard dimensions if possible. Order 5 to 10 percent more material than you estimate you will need to cover waste and damage.

If a licensed contractor will do some or all of your construction, ask that person to purchase materials for you at a professional discount.

construction tools

The tools required for your new screened room will depend on the extent of the project.

For a very simple job, such as fastening screening to an existing porch, you will need little more than a utility knife and staple gun. But for any project that requires construction, you'll need an assortment of basic carpentry tools.

The tools shown here are used repeatedly throughout this book's step-by-step projects. More-specialized tools are discussed in each project's instructions—rent or buy these as needed.

Though you can get by with hand tools for most jobs, power tools will let you do the job more quickly, easily, and accurately, especially if the structure is large.

TAPE MEASURE A 16- or 25-foot tape measure is sufficient for most jobs, but for laying out distances beyond 25 feet, choose a reel tape. A tape measure's end hook should be loosely riveted in order to adjust for precise "inside" and "outside" readings.

LEVEL To see if a horizontal surface is level, place a level on the surface. If the air bubble in the liquid enclosed in the center glass tubing lines up exactly between the two marks, the surface is level. When you hold the level vertically, the tubes near each end indicate plumb.

COMBINATION SQUARE A square helps you draw straight cutting lines across lumber; it also helps you check angles on assembled pieces of a structure. A combination square is the most versatile type of square because, in addition to checking both 45- and 90-degree angles, it can serve as a ruler and small level.

CHALK LINE A chalk line is ideal for marking long cutting lines on sheet materials and laying out reference lines on a wall, ceiling, or floor. To mark a line, stretch the chalk-covered cord taut between two points. Then lift and snap it down sharply.

PLUMB BOB To use a plumb bob, hang it by a string and maneuver

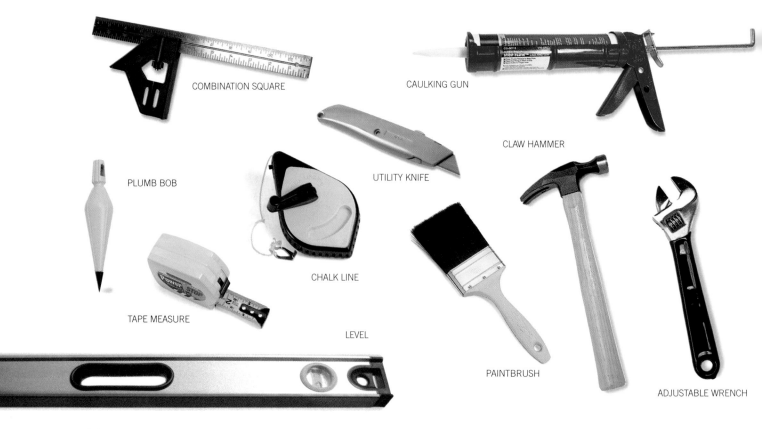

COMBINATION SQUARE

CAULKING GUN

CLAW HAMMER

PLUMB BOB

UTILITY KNIFE

CHALK LINE

TAPE MEASURE

LEVEL

PAINTBRUSH

ADJUSTABLE WRENCH

it until it almost touches the floor. When the weight stops swinging, you have perfect plumb. Mark the point on the floor (it helps to have a partner at the other end).

CLAW HAMMER Hammer faces are either flat or slightly convex. The convex, or bell-faced, type allows you to drive a nail flush without marring the wood's surface. Mesh-type faces are used for rough framing work—the mesh pattern helps guide the nails and keeps the face from glancing off large nailheads. Don't use this face for finish work because the pattern will imprint the surface.

UTILITY KNIFE A standard utility knife is helpful for many jobs, including cutting screening fabric, asphalt roofing, and more. Replace the blade frequently to ensure clean cuts.

PORTABLE CIRCULAR SAW Used for framing and many other construction jobs, this power saw allows you to make straight crosscuts much faster than with a handsaw and is unparalleled for ripping along the lengths of boards. The most common $7\frac{1}{4}$-inch model will go through surfaced 2-by framing lumber at any angle between 45 and 90 degrees.

MITER SAW Also called a chop saw, the miter saw excels at making clean, accurate angle cuts; if your project entails a lot of angles or requires a lot of detail work,

POWER DRILL/DRIVER

MITER SAW

PORTABLE CIRCULAR SAW

consider renting one. A 10-inch miter saw is standard. So-called compound miter saws cut angles in two directions at once, a feature that's sometimes handy for rafters or fancy trim. Sliding miter saws can cut stock up to about 1 foot wide.

POWER DRILL/DRIVER An electric drill is classified by the biggest bit shank it can accommodate in its chuck (jaws); the most common are $\frac{1}{4}$ inch, $\frac{3}{8}$ inch, and $\frac{1}{2}$ inch. For most jobs, a cordless $\frac{3}{8}$-inch variable-speed drill with an adjustable clutch is your best bet; it not only handles a wide range of bits and accessories, but it also makes an excellent power screwdriver. If you'll be driving many screws, a power drill/driver with screwdriver bits is a must.

ADJUSTABLE WRENCH For driving lag screws or tightening nuts and bolts, you'll need a 10- or 12-inch adjustable wrench, excellent for a range of jobs. If you have much of this work, consider getting a socket wrench with a set of sockets.

CAULKING GUN For applying caulk and other adhesives, use a caulking gun. A standard-sized one, which uses 10-ounce tubes, is the most convenient and easy-to-handle for most jobs.

PAINTBRUSH A 3- or 4-inch nylon-bristle brush works well for many types of applications. For painting trim, choose a 2-inch angled sash brush. Spread a brush's bristles to check for flagging (split ends) and springiness—signs of good quality.

building from foundation to rafters

Whether attached to a house or free-standing, all screened rooms are made up of the same basic components. This section lays out the techniques for creating one from scratch.

FOUNDATIONS

A screened structure is typically supported by a foundation—either a concrete slab or a series of footings and piers. The foundation distributes the weight of the structure and anchors it against settling, erosion, and wind lift. The foundation also isolates the walls or support posts from direct contact with the ground and thereby reduces the chances of decay and insect infestation.

Some gazebos or screened structures can directly sit on and fasten to an existing patio slab or deck, depending on the structure's weight and the deck's construction or the slab's thickness (see page 99). Building codes—which govern the size, depth, and makeup of foundations—determine whether or not this is viable.

Typically, a foundation's footing must extend into solid ground or rock. In cold-climate areas, it must extend below the frost line so it is not disturbed by frost heave.

LEDGERS

The floor or deck joists and roof rafters of a house-attached screened room usually connect to ledgers mounted on the house. As a general rule, a ledger is made from a piece of 2-by lumber of the same width as the material used for the joists or rafters.

Mounting the ledger is usually one of the first steps when building a house-attached structure; once the ledger is in place, it is easier to lay out the rest of the foundation. Procedures for mounting a ledger depend on the type of siding on the house.

Relatively flat siding can remain intact, but clapboard, beveled wood, metal, or vinyl siding should be cut away to allow a solid connection point for the ledger. Remove enough so you can tuck flashing behind the siding above the ledger and allow it to overhang the siding below the ledger, as shown below.

When cutting siding, adjust the blade of the circular saw so it cuts just the siding and not the sheathing underneath. Also, do not let the blade cut beyond the layout lines. If you are cutting vinyl siding, you can use a sharp utility knife instead.

MOUNTING A LEDGER A ledger should be affixed to strong parts of the house's framing, such as wall studs or second-floor joists. The strongest ledger connection relies on bolts that run through the ledger and the house sheathing and rim joist and then are fastened with nuts and washers affixed from the basement or crawl space. When access to the other side of the fasteners is not feasible, use lag screws instead of bolts. If it isn't possible to attach the ledger to a floor joist, fasten it to wall studs, generally located on 16-inch (sometimes 24-inch) centers and doubled up around doors,

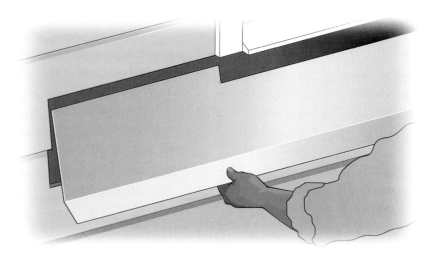

After cutting away a section of siding, slide metal flashing beneath the remaining siding. You may need to temporarily remove some siding nails first. Cut the flashing to fit around the door threshold, as shown. Apply caulk to the joint between the threshold and flashing.

TYING THE DECK TO THE HOUSE

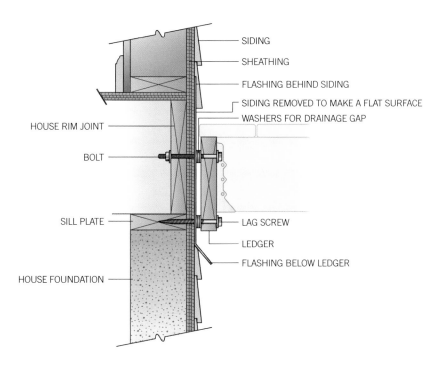

SIDING

SHEATHING

FLASHING BEHIND SIDING

SIDING REMOVED TO MAKE A FLAT SURFACE

WASHERS FOR DRAINAGE GAP

HOUSE RIM JOINT

BOLT

SILL PLATE

LAG SCREW

LEDGER

FLASHING BELOW LEDGER

HOUSE FOUNDATION

windows, and other openings. If placing a roof ledger beneath the eaves won't allow for enough headroom, set the ledger on the top plate and fasten it to the sides of the house rafters. Don't fasten a ledger to the eaves because the new roof might exert undue leverage on the house rafters.

Temporarily nail or brace the ledger in place, leveled and positioned at the desired height. Recheck for level, and then drill lag-screw or bolt pilot holes through the ledger and into the house's framing. Attach the ledger with $\frac{1}{2}$-inch-diameter lag screws or bolts, every 16 inches (or as specified by local codes).

It's a good idea to leave a space behind the ledger to allow for drainage. This is easily accomplished by placing three or four washers (galvanized or stainless steel) on each bolt, as shown above. As added protection, squirt some caulk into the holes before inserting bolts or lag screws.

FASTENING TO MASONRY WALLS

A ledger is anchored to a masonry wall with expanding anchor bolts. To attach a ledger, begin by marking a line across the wall for the ledger's top edge. Drill holes for the expanding anchors every 16 inches or as specified by local codes, insert the anchors, hold the ledger in place, and tap it with a hammer to indent the anchor locations on its back face. Remove the ledger and drill bolt holes where the bolt tips have left marks. Push or hammer the ledger back onto the bolts, recheck for level (making any needed adjust-

ments), add washers and nuts, and then tighten the bolts.

FLASHING A LEDGER Unless it is protected from rain by the house's eaves or a solid roof, a roof ledger fastened directly to a house with wood siding should be capped with galvanized metal flashing and caulked, as shown below, to prevent water from seeping in behind it. This is a job you must do before fastening the new structure's roof rafters in place.

To bend the sheet-metal flashing, make a form by clamping two 2 by 4s together on each side of the metal and hammer to create a sharp edge at each fold. Fit the flashing in place, caulk the top edge, and nail it with galvanized nails long enough to penetrate at least 1 inch into the structural members. Then caulk the nailheads. If the house is sided with shingles or lap siding, simply slip the metal's top edge up under the bottom edge of the shingles or siding as far as possible.

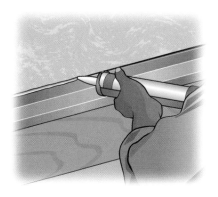

With the flashing seated firmly in the kerf and along the ledger, add a bead of caulk along the top edge of the flashing.

PLANNING THE STRUCTURE

When building a new screened room, you must size and space the support posts, beams, rafters, and other structural members to sufficiently bear loads (see below).

Once you've determined the locations of your structure's footings, you will need to transfer these measurements to the ground, deck, or patio. To ensure square corners, you'll need a helper and two tape measures. Use the 3-4-5 rule as follows (also see the illustration at the bottom of the facing page).

MAXIMUM RAFTER, JOIST, AND BEAM SPANS

An essential part of planning your project is determining the number, size, and spacing of rafters, joists, and beams according to the loads they will carry. The tables here give maximum recommended spans for quality framing lumber; always consult your local building department for code requirements.

(FOR DECK) BEAM SIZE	SPACING BETWEEN BEAMS (OR BEAM TO LEDGER)				
	6'	7-8'	9-10'	11'	12'
4 x 6	6'				
4 x 8	8'	7'	6'	6'	
DOUBLED 2 x 10	9'	8'	7'	6'	6'

(FOR ROOF) BEAM SIZE	SPACING BETWEEN BEAMS (OR BEAM TO LEDGER)				
	4'	8'	10'	12'	16'
2 x 6	7' 11"	7'	6' 6"	6' 3"	5' 6"
2 x 8	10' 6"	9' 6"	8' 6"	8'	7' 6"
2 x 10	13' 4"	12'	11' 3"	10' 6"	9' 6"
2 x 12	16' 3"	14' 6"	13' 6"	12' 9"	11' 6"
4 x 4	6' 11"	6'	5' 6"	5' 3"	4' 9"
4 x 6	10' 10"	9' 6"	8' 9"	8' 3"	7' 6"
4 x 8	14' 4"	12' 6"	11' 6"	11'	10'
DOUBLED 2 x 10	18' 3"	16'	14' 6"	14'	12' 6"

(FOR DECK) JOIST SIZE	JOIST SPACING		
	12"	16"	24"
2 x 6	10' 3"	9' 4"	8' 2"
2 x 8	13' 6"	12' 3"	10' 9"
2 x 10	17' 3"	15' 8"	13' 8"

(FOR ROOF) RAFTER SIZE	RAFTER SPACING		
	12"	16"	24"
2 x 4	9'	8' 3"	7' 3"
2 x 6	14' 6"	13'	11' 6"
2 x 8	19'	17'	15'

For a house-attached overhead, drive one nail into the ledger's end and then a second nail into the ledger exactly 3 feet away. Hook the end of one tape measure onto one nail and the end of the other tape measure onto the other nail. With your helper, pull out the tapes until the 4-foot mark on one tape meets the 5-foot mark on the other tape. The 4-foot mark perpendicular to the ledger will be the location of one corner post. Repeat on the other side to locate the other corner post.

For a free-standing structure, use the same method, but pound stakes into the ground instead of inserting nails into a ledger.

To refine your layout for precise placement of posts, set up batterboards. These will allow you to adjust and maintain taut perimeter lines while digging the footing holes. Batterboards are temporary attachment points for string lines. They are usually made with 1 by 4s or 2 by 4s, but you can use any scrap lumber available. Each batterboard consists of a crosspiece mounted on two stakes, which are cut with pointed bottoms so they can be driven easily into the ground. Locate batterboards about 18 inches from each corner stake.

If you're building off a house wall, run a plumb line down from each end of the ledger, and drive a nail partially into the wall about 1 inch above ground level. Run mason's lines from the nails to the opposite batterboards and then from batterboard to batterboard, as shown in the illustration at right.

Measure the diagonal distance between opposite corners and adjust the lines until the distances between both sets of corners are equal. When locating footing and post locations this way, remember that these lines show the perimeter—not the centers—of the posts and footings.

BUILDING ON AN EXISTING SLAB OR DECK

If you intend to build a screened structure on an existing deck or patio, be sure the patio or deck can support it without additional foundation work. Whether you can stand the structure directly on the slab or deck will depend on the slab's thickness or the deck's construction and the new structure's weight, as determined by codes.

For example, in some areas, a

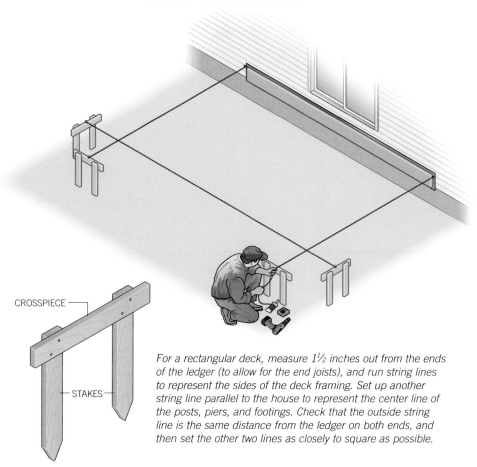

For a rectangular deck, measure 1½ inches out from the ends of the ledger (to allow for the end joists), and run string lines to represent the sides of the deck framing. Set up another string line parallel to the house to represent the center line of the posts, piers, and footings. Check that the outside string line is the same distance from the ledger on both ends, and then set the other two lines as closely to square as possible.

CROSSPIECE

STAKES

new structure can stand on a concrete slab if the slab is not less than 3½ inches thick and the

structure's posts don't support combined "live" and "dead" loads in excess of 750 pounds per post ("live" loads are forces from wind, people, and so forth; "dead" loads are from the structure's weight).

EXISTING SLAB To fasten directly to an existing slab (when allowed to by building codes), secure each post in a metal bolt-down post base such as the one shown on page 93. These post bases are made for both rough and surfaced 4-by-4, 4-by-6, and 6-by-6 posts. (For other post sizes, you can have bases specially fabricated by a sheet-metal shop or welder.)

Using a masonry bit in a power

ESTABLISHING SQUARE

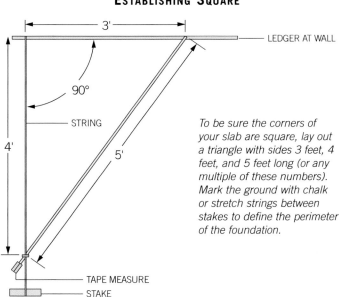

3'

90°

STRING

4'

5'

To be sure the corners of your slab are square, lay out a triangle with sides 3 feet, 4 feet, and 5 feet long (or any multiple of these numbers). Mark the ground with chalk or stretch strings between stakes to define the perimeter of the foundation.

LEDGER AT WALL

TAPE MEASURE

STAKE

drill, bore a hole in the center of each post base to receive a $\frac{1}{2}$-inch expanding anchor bolt. Insert the anchor bolt, add a post base, and then follow up with a washer and nut and tighten. To add the post, just cut its end square, place it in the stirrup of the post base, and nail the base to the post through pre-punched holes.

If the slab isn't thick enough or the overhead is too heavy, you'll have to either pour a new footing around the slab's perimeter or break out corner sections and pour deeper footings.

EXISTING DECK If allowed by your local building codes, you can bolt your new structure's posts to existing deck beams, joists, or other heavy structural members. The type of post base discussed above can be lag-screwed through decking to a joist or beam. Be sure to use lag screws that are long enough to penetrate the structural member by at least 2 inches.

POURING A FOUNDATION

Following are typical methods for pouring concrete foundations. Be aware that the foundations of some screened-room structures are integrated into the foundation of a patio or deck. For example, when a concrete patio is poured, deeper footings may be poured around the slab's perimeter to support an outdoor room. In the case of decks, structural members such as railing supports may be sized long enough to support

the roof of the screened room.

In many areas, you will need a building permit before you may pour a concrete foundation or slab. Check with your local building department, and be sure to follow the inspector's instructions to the letter.

Before doing the following work, read the section on Buying or Mixing Concrete on page 104.

FOOTINGS AND PIERS Waxed fiber tubes, readily available at home improvement centers and lumberyards, make forming and pouring footings and piers a relatively easy job. Be aware that, under some codes, you may be required to have the footings inspected before making the piers, or you may need to add several inches of

gravel to the bottom of each footing before adding concrete.

Dig and pour all footings and piers at one time, if possible. Be sure to have rebar and anchor bolts or post bases on hand, as you must add them to the concrete while it is still wet.

Lay out the footings as discussed on page 98. The spacing between footings for support posts is determined by post placements, which are a factor of beam spans (see the chart on page 98).

In areas with freezing winters, a concrete footing usually must extend several inches below the frost line (the depth at which soil freezes in a given area). At minimum, a footing should be 8 inches thick and twice as wide as the wall or posts it will support.

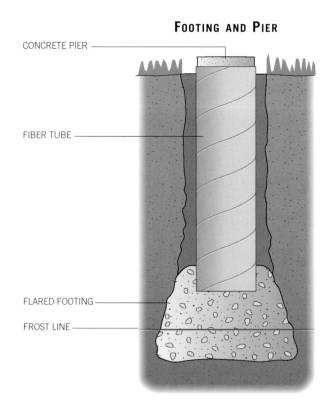

FOOTING AND PIER

CONCRETE PIER

FIBER TUBE

FLARED FOOTING

FROST LINE

How to Pour a Footing and Pier

1 **Dig a flared hole**, sized as required by code, using a clamshell digger or a power hole auger.

2 **Cut a length** of waxed fiber tube long enough to extend 2 inches above grade and 2 inches into the flared footing at the bottom of the hole.

3 **Level and suspend** the tube in the center of the hole by screwing it to temporary braces. Begin to fill it with concrete.

4 **Fill the flared section** of the footing and the bottom 2 feet of the tube with concrete. Using a piece of wood, agitate the mix to remove any air pockets. Repeat every 2 feet, until the tube is slightly overfilled. Smooth the surface by moving a short 2 by 4 from side to side.

5 **Add rebar** according to code requirements, typically two pieces of #4 rebar spaced about 2 inches from the fiber tube. Each should be long enough to reach from the bottom of the footing to about 2 inches below the pier's surface. Insert an anchor bolt, post base, or short rebar "pin" for centering the post, and check it for alignment.

6 **Allow the concrete to cure** for at least two days, keeping it damp. Remove the temporary braces, backfill the hole with dirt, and cut away the exposed fiber tubing.

CONCRETE SLABS A concrete slab may be cast at the same time as the footings or after the footings have set up. The slab's overall dimensions, of course, will be determined by the size of your new structure.

Before casting the concrete, place any plumbing or electrical conduit. After casting the slab, do not allow the surface to dry too quickly or it may crack. Spray it with a light mist of water, cover it with plastic sheeting, and allow it to cure for three days (or longer in cold weather).

HOW TO POUR A SLAB

1 Mark the ground with chalk or stretch mason's lines between batterboards (as discussed on page 99) to define the foundation's perimeter. A rectangular slab should have corners at precise 90-degree angles. To ensure the corners are square, lay out a triangle with sides 3 feet, 4 feet, and 5 feet long (or any multiple of these numbers).

2 To excavate for a large slab, you can hire a backhoe, as shown here. A 4-inch-thick slab is generally ample; in areas where frost or drainage may be a problem, the slab should be poured over a 4-to-6-inch gravel bed, so dig deeply enough to accommodate this.

3 Build temporary forms from scrap lumber nailed securely to stakes. Make sure their top edges are level to expedite finishing the concrete later. Install the gravel bed. Reinforce the area as required by code (typically with $\frac{1}{2}$-inch reinforcing bar around the perimeter and 6-inch-square 10-10 welded-wire mesh within the slab area). Support the mesh about 2 inches above the base with small pieces of brick or block.

4 Thoroughly dampen the soil or gravel. Beginning at one corner, place and spread the concrete. Work the mix up against the form and compact it into all corners with a shovel or mortar hoe by pushing (not dragging) it. Don't overwork the material or you may cause the heavy aggregate to sink to the bottom.

5 Move a straight 2 by 4 across the top of the forms to level the concrete, using a zigzag sawing motion. Fill any voids with more concrete and re-level.

6 To smooth the surface, move a darby (which you may want to rent) in overlapping arcs, and then repeat with overlapping straight side-to-side strokes. Keep the tool flat, and don't let it dig in. After the water sheen disappears from the concrete, but before the surface becomes really stiff, smooth it once more with a wood or magnesium hand float.

7 Install anchor bolts where required by your plan, typically every 3 to 4 feet, while the concrete is still plastic.

BUYING OR MIXING CONCRETE

Basic concrete is composed of Portland cement, sand, gravel (also called aggregate), and water. Portland cement is the glue that holds the mix together. The more cement, the stronger the concrete will be. If you are mixing a small amount of concrete or mortar and want to strengthen it, simply add a shovel or two of cement. When ordering from a ready-mix company, specify how much cement you want: A "six-bag mix" contains six bags of cement per yard of concrete, making it strong enough for most projects. For more about the proper mixture of concrete, see "Mixing Your Own" on the following page.

If you live in an area with freezing winters, consider ordering air-entrained concrete, which contains tiny air bubbles. The bubbles lend the concrete a bit of flexibility, so it is less likely to crack in cold weather. Air-entrained concrete is available only from a concrete truck.

If freezing weather is possible on the day of the pour, you can order an accelerating additive, which makes the concrete harden more quickly. If the weather is hot and dry, consider adding a retardant, which slows the drying time. If the concrete sets too fast, you may not have enough time to adequately finish the surface.

ORDERING GUIDELINES Begin by taking careful measurements of the area to be filled. A discrepancy of only $\frac{1}{2}$ inch can make a big difference in the amount of concrete you need.

When ordering, tell the supplier the dimensions—the square footage and depth. A reliable supplier will calculate how much you will need, but you will want to double-check these calculations against your own.

Concrete is usually sold by the cubic yard, just called a yard. A yard of concrete (or sand or gravel) fills an area 3 feet by 3 feet by 3 feet. For a small project such as a pier footing, you may choose to measure cubic footage instead; bags of dry-mix concrete often include cubic footage on the package, as well.

Using a calculator, it's easy to figure out concrete needs. For a rectangular slab or footing, multiply the width in feet times the length in feet times the thickness in inches. Divide the result by 12 to get the number of cubic feet. Divide that number by 27 to get the number of cubic yards. For example, if a slab measures 20 feet by 30 feet and its thickness is $3\frac{1}{2}$ inches:

$$20 \times 30 \times 3.5 = 2,100$$
$$2,100 \div 12 = 175 \text{ cubic feet}$$
$$175 \div 27 = 6.48 \text{ yards}$$

Adding about 10 percent for waste, you would order a little more than 7 yards.

If you need more than $\frac{1}{4}$ yard of concrete, ordering ready-mixed concrete is usually worth the extra expense. A 60-pound sack of dry-mix concrete makes about $\frac{1}{2}$ cubic foot, meaning that you would need to mix 52 bags to make just one yard of concrete. Many ready-mixed-concrete

With a power mixer you can reduce physical exertion. You can also save money by buying dry ingredients separately and mixing them yourself, but be sure to measure the relative proportions carefully.

companies will not deliver less than a yard of concrete. Others have special trucks designed to mix smaller amounts at the job site. If one company won't deliver a small amount for you, just keep calling around.

Before arranging for concrete to be delivered, familiarize yourself with the steps on pages 102–103; you won't have time to read instructions once the work begins. If the truck driver has to wait more than half an hour, you will usually incur extra expense, so plan to move the concrete quickly.

- Have all tools on hand, including two wheelbarrows.
- Be ready with at least one reliable helper, preferably two.
- If you want a smooth steel-trowel finish, line up an experienced concrete finisher.
- Install any isolation joints and wire reinforcement beforehand.
- Run and test wheelbarrow paths, and make sure the forms are securely anchored. Install all forms and guides.
- If required, make sure the building inspector has checked the site before you pour.
- If your design includes metal post anchors that will be embedded in the slab, have them on hand.

MIXING YOUR OWN If you want to mix concrete in small batches or are unable to find a company that will do that for you, you can rent

Empty a full bag of dry, premixed concrete into a mortar tub. (If you try to use only a partial bag, you may not pour out the properly balanced mixture of ingredients.) Mix the dry ingredients together, and then pour about 90 percent of the suggested amount of water into a small crater in the middle. Pull the dry ingredients into the water with the hoe, and mix carefully. Add small amounts of water until the mixture is plastic.

an electric-powered concrete mixer. Transporting the sand, gravel, and bagged cement requires a pickup truck with a bed that seals tight.

To mix your own concrete for footings and piers, use 1 part Portland cement, 2 parts clean river sand, and 3 parts gravel (maximum of 1-inch diameter and specially washed for concrete mixing). Add clean water, a little at a time, as you mix. The concrete should be plastic and not runny. You can also use dry mix or transit mix, which contain the same proportions of cement, sand, and gravel detailed above. Tumble,

adding water slowly, for two or three minutes, and then pour.

Concrete hardens because the powder-like cement and water form an adhesive that binds the sand and gravel together. Too much water thins or dilutes this adhesive paste and weakens its cementing qualities; too little makes it stiff and unworkable.

If the batch is too stiff, add water one cup at a time, and continue mixing until it's right. If it is too soupy, add small amounts of sand and gravel. Note that concrete changes consistency radically when you add even small amounts of any ingredient.

FINISHING WOOD PARTS

Though finishing your structure before you've built it may be the furthest thing from your mind, it is often much easier to finish some of the material before it is assembled.

Most wood used outdoors needs a finish to preserve its beauty and protect it from decay. Whether you choose a water repellent, a semitransparent or solid-color stain, or paint, test it on a sample board first to make sure you like the way it looks. Follow label directions carefully and allow the wood to dry thoroughly before deciding.

From top to bottom: Unfinished redwood; with clear water sealer; tinted oil-based repellent; gray semitransparent stain; and red solid-color stain.

Water repellents (water sealers) help keep wood from warping and cracking. They may be clear or slightly tinted; the clear sorts do not color the wood but let it fade gradually to gray. You can buy either oil- or water-based products, many of which include UV blockers and mildewcides.

Don't use clear-surface finishes such as spar varnish or polyurethane on outdoor lumber. In addition to being costly, they wear quickly and are very hard to renew.

Readily available in both water- and oil-based versions, semitransparent stains contain enough pigment to tint the wood's surface with just one coat while still letting the natural grain show through. You'll find grays and wood tones as well as products to "revive" an unpainted structure's natural wood color or dress up pressure-treated wood.

To cover a structure in a solid color, you can choose either stain or paint. Stains for siding or decking are essentially thin paints that cover the wood grain completely. For custom tints, you can usually mix any paint color you choose into this base.

Paints cover wood in an opaque coat of muted or vibrant color. Because they hide defects so thoroughly, they allow you to use lower grades of lumber where strength is not a consideration. Most painters recommend a two-step procedure for outdoor structures. First, apply an alkyd- or oil-based prime coat, and then follow it with one or two topcoats of water-based (latex) enamel. Ideally, the primer should cover all surfaces of the lumber (including the inner faces of built-up posts, beams, or rafters), so in this case you will want to prime before assembly. You can apply topcoats after the structure is completed or apply topcoats before assembly and touch up after construction is complete.

Heavy-bodied stains may be brushed or sprayed on; paint can be applied with a brush, roller, or spray gun. It's easiest to spray complex shapes such as lath and lattice.

POSTS AND BEAMS

Most screened rooms utilize post-and-beam construction. The floor of the room is often a basic, low-level deck with decking boards supported by joists that sit on beams, which are held by posts. The posts may be short ones that hold only the deck beams or longer ones that extend to support the roof structure.

POSTS AND COLUMNS Posts for screened enclosures are usually solid lumber such as 4 by 4s or 6 by 6s, though, in some cases, they're built up from more than one size of lumber. Any post that may touch the ground should be pressure-treated for decay resistance. Posts offer plenty of latitude for detailing—you can route them, cut them, build up interesting profiles, or nail on decorative pieces to add visual interest.

BEAMS (OR "GIRDERS") Beams may be solid lumber or built-up lengths of 2-by dimension lumber nailed together. If an especially large beam is required, a built-up one is easiest to handle because it can be assembled on the ground near its final destination. The trade-off, of course, is that it involves more labor. Where highly visible, a single solid beam is generally favored.

The typical built-up beam is made from two thicknesses of 2-by lumber with ½-inch-thick spacers between the boards, producing a beam that matches the width of a 4-by post. (Note that, in strength, this is equivalent to a 3-inch-thick beam.)

You can also build up a 3-inch-wide beam without spacers. Just nail together the two boards by driving 10d galvanized nails along both sides every 16 inches, stag-

gering them as shown above. Apply a bead of silicone caulk to the joint between the boards to prevent moisture from seeping between them. Be sure the crowns (a crown is the "high" side of a curve or warp along the edge of a

board) on the pieces align; then, when you mount the beam on the posts, place the crown side up.

POST-AND-BEAM CONNECTIONS You can fasten a beam to a post using any of the methods shown below.

BUILT-UP BEAM WITH SPACERS

12"

12d NAILS

½" PLYWOOD SPACER

BUILT-UP BEAM WITHOUT SPACERS

CAULK ALONG JOINT

10d NAILS

16"

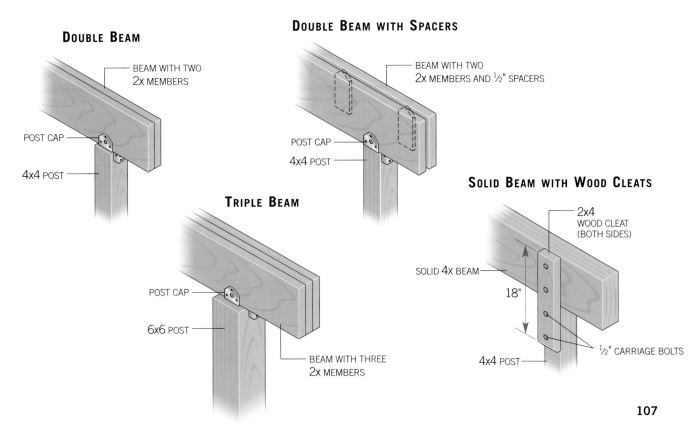

DOUBLE BEAM

BEAM WITH TWO 2x MEMBERS

POST CAP

4x4 POST

DOUBLE BEAM WITH SPACERS

BEAM WITH TWO 2x MEMBERS AND ½" SPACERS

POST CAP

4x4 POST

TRIPLE BEAM

POST CAP

6x6 POST

BEAM WITH THREE 2x MEMBERS

SOLID BEAM WITH WOOD CLEATS

2x4 WOOD CLEAT (BOTH SIDES)

SOLID 4x BEAM

18"

4x4 POST

½" CARRIAGE BOLTS

MEASURING POST HEIGHTS

Accurate measurement of post heights is critical when building a screened structure because precisely measured posts will determine the structure's ultimate stability. Nearly all of the projects in this book are structures that utilize both beams and joists and/or rafters; if your plan is different, you can adjust the directions to accommodate the slope of your land, your posts' heights, and similar factors.

When building a house-attached structure, first work on the posts farthest from the house. For a free-standing structure, begin with the posts that support opposite edges and corners and then do any intermediate posts.

Measuring for posts of free-standing structures is different from that for house-attached screened rooms in only one respect: With an attached room, you have already defined the height of the roof at the ledger line along the wall. For a free-standing structure, you will erect a post at a slightly taller height than desired, mark the height you wish on the post, and work from that as you would from a ledger on a house wall.

ROOF PITCH AND MINIMUM HEIGHT

Many roofing materials require a certain pitch in order to shed rain effectively. Don't forget to allow for rain runoff in whichever roofing you choose. For typical pitches, see page 118.

Beams beneath the deck or floor should clear the ground with a couple of inches to spare to prevent moisture damage from heavy rains or snow melt-off.

The minimum clearance for beams in an occupied space is normally 7 feet to prevent people from bumping their heads.

MARKING AND CUTTING POSTS

The method pictured for marking and cutting posts will work whether the posts are intended for a screened room's deck, floor, or roof. You can adapt these directions to fit your situation.

If you are using pressure-treated posts, place the uncut ends into the post bases—but only if they are square. Use a combination square to check; if they are not, cut just enough off the bottom to make surfaces square. Coat the cut surface with a water-repellent preservative before setting the posts in place.

RAISING POSTS

Posts can be quite heavy, so you'll need a helper to place them. Before positioning a post, drive two stakes into the ground and nail a brace made from a 1 by 2 or 1 by 3 to each stake. Position the stakes so the braces are at a 45-degree angle when midway up the post. Seat the post in the anchor, and check for plumb. Nail the braces to the post, and then nail or lag-screw the post to its base. Drive additional nails into each brace until the beams are seated.

HOW TO MARK AND CUT POSTS

1 Cut two posts 6 to 12 inches longer than the estimated finish lengths (the post shown here is for the floor of a screened room). Fit the base of each post in its anchor, and use a carpenter's level to check two adjacent sides for plumb. Attach temporary 1-by-4 braces to two adjacent sides, and secure them with screws to stakes in the ground and with clamps to the posts.

2 Drive nails through the post brackets and into the posts, using nails recommended by the manufacturer of the post bases, when all posts are plumbed and aligned along a string line.

3 To mark each post at the spot that is level with the top of the ledger, place a carpenter's level on the straightest 2 by 4 you can find. Set one end of the 2 by 4 on top of the ledger, and then adjust the other end along the post until it is level. Mark the post at the bottom of the 2 by 4. If the posts are too far from the ledger for this method, use a water level.

4 Place a short piece of joist stock under the mark on one post, and then mark the post under it. If the joists will rest on top of (rather than beside) the beam, set a piece of beam stock under this line, and mark under it. If you're measuring a post for the roof, subtract any drop for roof

pitch. This final line is where you need to cut the post. Repeat this process for each post, or use a straight 2 by 4 and a level to transfer the mark.

5 **Use a combination square** to transfer the cut line to all four sides of each post. Set the blade of a circular saw to cut as deeply as possible. For a 4-by-4 post, you will need to cut the post twice, on opposite sides. For a 6-by-6 post, cut along the line on all four sides, and then finish the cut with a reciprocating saw or handsaw.

SEATING BEAMS Setting up a low beam (one that's intended to support decking or a screened room's floor) is a relatively easy job, as shown below. With a helper, just lift and set it into post caps mounted at the top of each post. Slide it one direction or the other to align it with your layout, and then nail the post caps to the side of the beam with nails recommended by the post-cap manufacturer.

Setting a beam on top of tall posts is a little more difficult. When you get to this point in construction, ask an able-bodied neighbor or two for help. Drag the

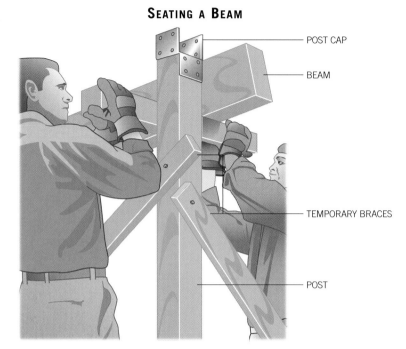

POST CAP

BEAM

TEMPORARY BRACES

POST

Align the beam with string lines representing the edges of the screened room's floor. If the beam is too long, overlap it the same distance on each end (so the crown is centered), then cut both ends to length, and seal it.

beam into rough position next to the posts, and slip a short length of 4 by 4 under one end of the beam. Raise that end of the beam, and maneuver it into the post caps. Drive in one nail part way so the beam won't slide off the post when you lift the other end. Then lift and place the other end. Last, nail the post caps to the beam as recommended by the post-cap manufacturer.

BRACING POSTS Some codes require that certain post-and-beam designs have crossbracing for lateral stability during high winds or seismic events. Typically at heights of less than 12 feet, only outside posts on unattached sides of the substructure need crossbracing. Free-standing structures with posts taller than 3 feet usually require bracing, as well. As shown at right, use 2 by 4s for bracing across distances less than 8 feet and 2 by 6s for greater distances. Bolt or lag-screw the crossbraces to the posts.

For tall posts, mark each crossbrace in position, and then cut them on the ground. After treating braces with a finish, temporarily nail them in place, drill pilot holes for bolts or lag screws, squirt the holes with wood finish, and then permanently fasten them with the bolts or lag screws.

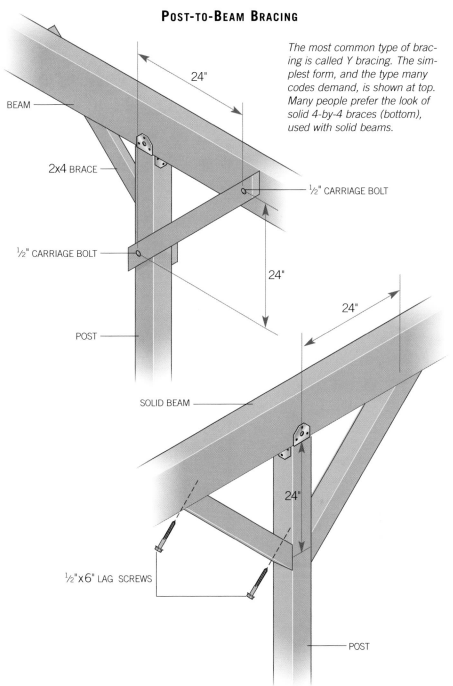

POST-TO-BEAM BRACING

The most common type of bracing is called Y bracing. The simplest form, and the type many codes demand, is shown at top. Many people prefer the look of solid 4-by-4 braces (bottom), used with solid beams.

BEAM

24"

2x4 BRACE

½" CARRIAGE BOLT

½" CARRIAGE BOLT

POST

24"

24"

SOLID BEAM

24"

½"x6" LAG SCREWS

POST

HANGING JOISTS

Joists, the structural members that support decking or flooring, are typically spaced 16 inches apart from center to center and are supported by beams and/or a ledger at one end. When attached to a ledger, they're normally mounted with joist hangers. They may overhang a beam by a foot or two and be toenailed or fastened to it with hurricane or seismic ties. Or they may be installed so that they are even with the beams and attached with joist hangers.

Choose joist stock carefully.

Look for the straightest boards you can find, and always install them with the crown side (the "high" side of an edgeline warp) facing up.

Although you may have to square the ends where they meet the ledger, you do not need to cut individual joists to length at this stage. Instead, cut them only after you've installed all the joists. If your design calls for doubled joists, maintain the on-center spacing by locating the center in the gap between the doubled joists.

Always use joist hangers that are made for the size of joists you are using, and attach them with the type and quantity of fasteners specified by the manufacturer.

How to Install Joists

1 **Drill three pilot holes** through each joist and into the ledger to prevent splitting, starting with the outside joists, and then fasten each joist to an end of the ledger with 16d galvanized nails. Attach reinforcing angle brackets to the inside corners.

2 **Square up** the end joists at the ledger and the beam, either by using string lines or by measuring the diagonals to make sure they're equal (see page 99). The end of the beam should be flush with the outer edges of the joists. If you need to cut the beam, use a square to mark the cut line, and then make the cut with a circular saw or reciprocating saw. Trim the bottom corner at an angle for appearance, if you wish.

3 **Measure and mark** the ledger for the locations of the other joists. Hook a tape measure over the outside face of an end joist, and then mark along the top of the ledger according to the planned on-center spacing (typically 16 inches). Using a square, make a vertical line on the ledger at each mark, to represent the edge of a joist; mark an X alongside it to indicate where to place the joist.

4 **Mount joist hangers** on the ledger using a short piece of joist stock as a guide to keep the joist tops level with the top of the ledger. Fasten one side of each hanger, then the other. Set a joist into a hanger, make sure the joist is perpendicular to the ledger, and then nail through the joist hanger into the joist on both sides. Repeat this procedure with the remaining joists.

5 **Attach the joists** to the beam(s) when they are all square and properly aligned. As shown here, an easy and secure method is to use seismic or hurricane ties to fasten them.

6 **Measure out** from the ledger along each end joist, mark the proper length, and then snap a chalk line between these marks across the tops of the joists. Using a square and a pencil, transfer the chalk marks onto the faces of each joist. Then cut each joist to length with a circular saw. If your design includes a rim joist, have a helper hold it in place so you can nail it to the joist ends. Use 16d galvanized nails.

WORKING WITH TREATED WOOD

Treated wood is required by many building codes for certain uses. Although safer products are becoming more readily available, certain types of treated wood still contain ingredients that are toxic. For this reason, it is wise to take the following precautions when working with any wood that has been treated:

■ Use treated lumber only where its protection is needed, such as for posts, ledgers, beams, and joists.

■ Only use treated wood that is visibly free of surface residue.

■ Clean up all sawdust and waste pieces from your work site promptly.

■ Never burn or recycle treated wood. Dispose of unwanted pieces in the regular trash.

■ Always wear a dust mask, protective eyewear, and leather gloves when cutting treated wood.

■ Seal the wood with a water repellent at a minimum of every two years.

INSTALLING DECKING

Many screened rooms utilize conventional 2-by-6 or 2-by-4 decking—or 2-by-6 composite decking—for their floors. Decking can be fastened to the floor joists with nails, decking screws, or special decking clips or fasteners that don't show on the surface.

Gaps between decking boards are necessary for drainage if the floor will be exposed to the weather. A typical gap is ⅛ inch; many deck builders use a 16d galvanized nail as a spacer. To prevent bugs from entering through the gaps, stretch and staple screening fabric across the tops of the joists before installing the deck boards.

Fasteners should be driven through the decking at each joist location. Butt joints, where board ends meet, must be centered over joists. When driving screws or nails at board ends, drill pilot holes first to avoid splitting the wood. Install screws or nails 1 inch from each edge of the decking, and align the fastener pattern along each joist. Drive nails flush with the top of the decking, but avoid crushing the wood—the dents will show. If a board is slightly warped, you can drive a chisel into the joist and use it as a lever to pull the board into alignment.

As you approach the last several rows of decking, adjust the spacing slightly so the final board will fit evenly (you may have to

Clockwise from above: Decking can be fastened to floor joists with nails, special decking fasteners, or decking screws (the easiest of the three options for wood). If a board is slightly warped, pull it into alignment by driving a chisel into the joist and using it as a lever. To trim wood or composite boards (as shown at right), snap a chalk line, and cut them with a power circular saw.

rip small amounts off the final three or four rows). Let the boards run long at the sides of the deck, snap a chalk line, and then trim them all at once with a power circular saw. If you are concerned about being able to make a straight cut, tack a 1 by 4 to the deck surface to guide the saw. If you're installing composite decking, clean up the edges with a power sander.

INSTALLING RAFTERS

Most screened rooms have rafters that distribute roofing loads across beams. Rafters must support their own weight plus the weight of the roof covering without sagging or twisting. Their sizes are determined by code (see page 98).

Installation methods are similar to those for installing floor or ceiling joists (see page 112). The main difference is that rafters are usually pitched at an angle so the roof will shed rain.

RAFTER CONNECTIONS Rafters can be supported by beams and ledgers using any one of several methods. Note that rafters can either sit on top of beams and ledgers, as shown at top right, or connect to the faces of these supports.

GAZEBO HUBS Most gazebos have a center point—or "hub"—where roof rafters meet. The hub makes it easy to join the rafter ends, which are often cut at compound angles. Typical hubs are shown on this page.

RAFTER CONNECTION

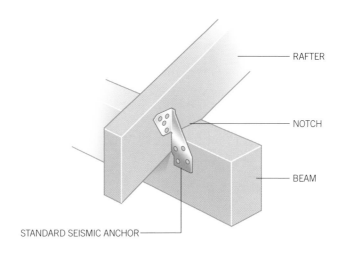

RAFTER

NOTCH

BEAM

STANDARD SEISMIC ANCHOR

HUB STYLES

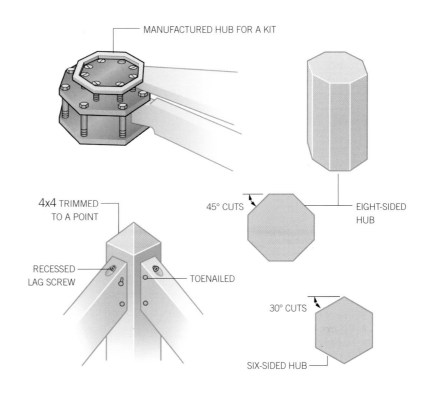

MANUFACTURED HUB FOR A KIT

4x4 TRIMMED TO A POINT

RECESSED LAG SCREW

TOENAILED

45° CUTS

EIGHT-SIDED HUB

30° CUTS

SIX-SIDED HUB

CUTTING RAFTERS FOR A HOUSE-ATTACHED SHED ROOF Fitting sloping rafters in place is an exacting operation. Carpenters use any one of several methods, but you're most likely to do a good job by following the old-fashioned method of cutting one rafter to fit and then using it as a template for the rest. The procedure used for a house-attached roof is shown in the step-by-step on page 116.

HOW TO CUT AND FIT RAFTERS

1 **Lay a rafter board** so it rests on its edge on both the ledger and the beam parallel to the ledger.

2 **Force the rafter's tip** snugly against the house wall. Using a block of wood as a ruler, mark the ends for cutting.

3 **Cut the triangular piece** off the rafter end that rests on the ledger and off the end that rests on the beam, as shown.

4 **Cut notches** where the rafter rests on the ledger and on the beam. Place the rafter in several positions along the ledger and the beam to check for fit.

5 **Mark and cut** the remaining rafters, using this rafter as a template. Before fastening them in place, treat them with an appropriate wood finish (see page 106).

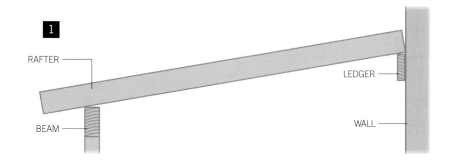

1

RAFTER

LEDGER

BEAM

WALL

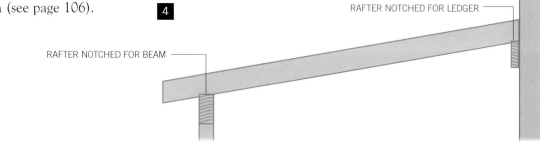

2

MARK ALONG STICK TO
CREATE TEMPLATE

MARKED WITH TEMPLATE,
TO BE REMOVED

NOTCH TO BE REMOVED

3

TRIANGULAR BLOCK REMOVED;
USE AS TEMPLATE

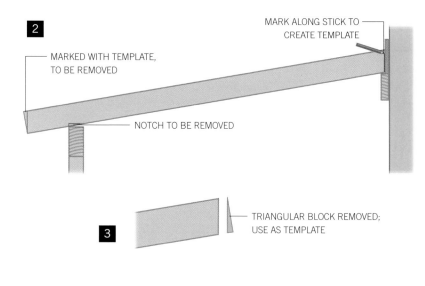

4

RAFTER NOTCHED FOR LEDGER

RAFTER NOTCHED FOR BEAM

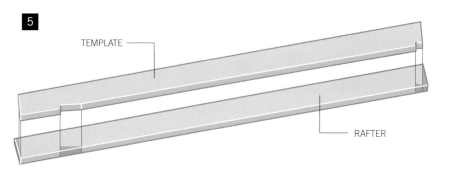

5

TEMPLATE

RAFTER

BRACING RAFTERS If rafter spans are long, the rafters can twist or buckle unless they are crossbraced or blocked. The width of the rafters determines the blocking; 2-by-12 to 2-by-8 rafters require more blocking than 2 by 6s. Blocking is typically determined by local codes.

A common method of bracing is shown at right. If rafter spans are less than 8 feet, headers nailed across rafter ends are adequate for stability. Stagger the blocks from one side to the other, and then face-nail them using 16d galvanized nails.

STAGGERED BLOCKING OVER A BEAM

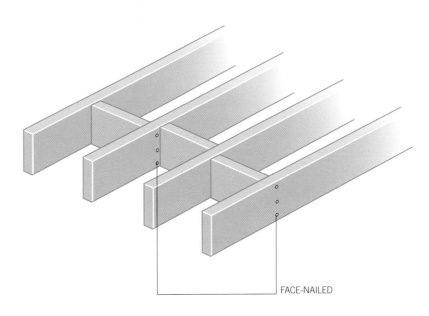

FACE-NAILED

BUILDING A GABLED ROOF

Building this type of roof is difficult, somewhat dangerous work that should be left in the hands of a professional if you are not a very experienced do-it-yourselfer. The primary elements of a gabled roof are shown at right.

This type of structure usually requires ceiling joists, placed on their edges and nailed to the top plates of the walls. These joists support the load of the ceiling materials below and help to permanently brace the walls against the thrust of the rafters above. Joists normally span the width of the structure, resting on opposite walls or supports; they may also rest on a beam or bearing wall at the center.

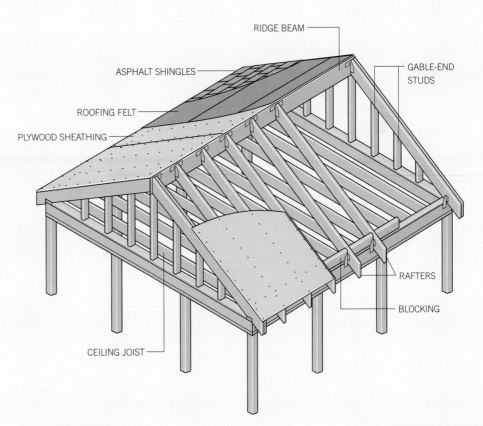

RIDGE BEAM

ASPHALT SHINGLES

GABLE-END STUDS

ROOFING FELT

PLYWOOD SHEATHING

RAFTERS

BLOCKING

CEILING JOIST

ROOFING BASICS

While some screened rooms have open-style framing with screened, plastic, or glass panels, most have solid roofs. By far, the most common is asphalt-fiberglass shingle roofing, for which installation instructions are provided here. Other roofing materials—including tile, concrete, metal, or glass—should be installed by an experienced contractor.

The illustration below outlines the parts of a typical roof. Though many screened-room roofs are much simpler than this—without valleys or ridges, for example—a complex patio or gazebo roof could involve any or all of these features.

ABOUT ROOF PITCH Appropriate choices for roofing material are determined by roof pitch, or slope. Roof pitch refers to the vertical rise measured against a horizontal distance of 12 inches. The term "4 in 12," applied to a roof, tells you that the roof rises vertically 4 inches for every 12 horizontal inches. Very low-sloped roofs measure only 1 in 12 or 2 in 12; steeply sloped roofs range from 12 in 12 (a 45-degree angle) up to 20 in 12. Ordinarily, a do-it-yourselfer can work safely on a single-story roof with a slope up to 5 in 12.

Some materials offer more protection than others. The steeper a roof's pitch, the more water will roll off without penetrating it. Asphalt shingles, wood shingles, aluminum shingles, tile, and slate are appropriate for roofs with a 4-in-12 or greater slope. With extra underlayment, asphalt shingles can be applied to 2-in-12 slopes; wood shingles and shakes and tile to 3 in 12. Do-it-yourself plastic and aluminum panels work well on slopes as gradual as 2 in 12—but don't expect them to hold off all rain. Asphalt ("tar") and gravel roofing can go on flat roofs; roll roofing can go on slopes of 1 in 12.

INSTALLING SHEATHING On house roofs, as shown below, asphalt shingles are normally applied over a solid deck of plywood sheathing with an underlayment of 15-pound roofing felt. Screened rooms and gazebos differ from most house roofs in that many don't have ceilings to hide the roof's structure when viewed from inside. For that reason, solid sheathing is typically preferred. In fact, you may want to choose a high-grade material such as tongue-and-groove 2-by-6 sheathing or a material that has a

ASPHALT-SHINGLE ROOF CONSTRUCTION

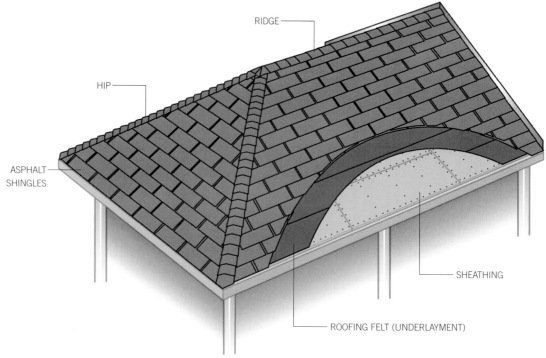

RIDGE

HIP

ASPHALT SHINGLES

SHEATHING

ROOFING FELT (UNDERLAYMENT)

good, paintable side or a resawn texture. (To cut down on neck strain, stain or prime and paint before installation.)

To install plywood sheathing, stagger $\frac{5}{8}$-inch 4-by-8-foot panels horizontally across the rafters, centering the panel ends on the rafters (leave $\frac{1}{8}$ inch between edges and $\frac{1}{16}$ inch between ends of adjoining panels for expansion). Nail panels to the rafters with 8d galvanized common or box nails, spacing the nails every 6 inches along panel ends and every 12 inches at intermediate supports. Let the panels run beyond the roof's edge, snap a chalk line along the length, and cut off the overhang with a circular saw (set the blade so it just cuts through the panels).

ROLLING OUT THE UNDERLAYMENT

Underlayment, also called roofing felt, is required beneath asphalt shingles and some other materials. To cover a roofing deck with it, start by measuring the roof carefully and snapping horizontal chalk lines to align the rows of underlayment. Snap the first line $33\frac{5}{8}$ inches above the eaves (this allows for a $\frac{3}{8}$-inch overhang). Then snap succeeding chalk lines at 34 inches to allow for a 2-inch overlap between strips of felt.

When applying the felt, start at the eaves and roll out the strips toward the ridge or top edge. Trim the felt flush at the gable overhang, and overlap it 6 inches at the ridge and any hips or valleys.

INSTALLING UNDERLAYMENT

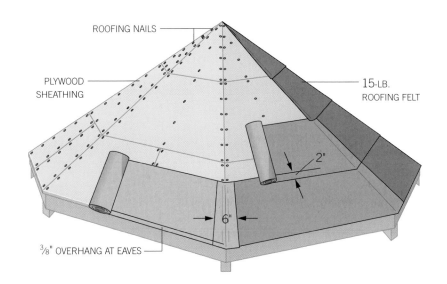

ROOFING NAILS

PLYWOOD SHEATHING

15-LB. ROOFING FELT

2"

6"

$\frac{3}{8}$" OVERHANG AT EAVES

INSTALLING DRIP EDGES

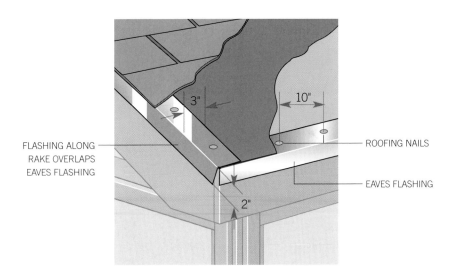

3"

10"

FLASHING ALONG RAKE OVERLAPS EAVES FLASHING

ROOFING NAILS

EAVES FLASHING

2"

Where two strips meet vertically, overlap them by 4 inches.

Drive in just enough roofing nails or staples to hold down the felt until the roofing is in place.

INSTALLING FLASHING Flashing protects a roof at its most vulnerable points: where the roof connects to the house, along eaves, in valleys, and anywhere else water could seep into the sheathing. Flashing is most commonly made of a malleable 28-gauge galvanized sheet metal, plastic, or aluminum. You can buy preformed flashings for drip edges and valleys or make your own. A typical method of flashing is shown in the illustration above.

INSTALLING GUTTERS

To protect your screened room from water and debris running off the roof, you will need to install gutters. The best time to install them is before you roof.

You may be able to save on labor costs by installing your gutters yourself, but this usually isn't worth the effort. The most popular gutters today, "seamless gutters," are extruded from metal (typically aluminum with a baked-on finish) "coil" stock on site by a gutter fabricator. They are secure and relatively inexpensive even with the cost of installation.

The gutter systems you can buy at home improvement centers and install yourself, known as "sectional" gutter systems, are typically made of vinyl, pre-painted steel, galvanized steel, or painted aluminum. With these, you can buy preformed channels from 10 to 22 feet long and any of the many different components that join onto the channels, as shown in the illustration below. One typical vinyl system has elbows, connectors, and other components with silicone gaskets that form watertight seals. You simply plug together the system. Other types are glued together with PVC cement.

Gutters are attached along a house's eaves by any of several types of straps, brackets, and hangers. Of these, bracket hangers, screwed to the fascia or rafter tails, tend to be the preferred method. But if the roof doesn't have these support members, a strap—ideally mounted beneath the shingles—is the method that is most commonly used.

Downspouts are connected to the gutter with a series of elbows and then secured to the house with wide straps. You will want to install one hanger for every 3 feet of gutter and three straps for every 10 feet of downspout.

Before hanging the gutter, assemble the parts on the ground as much as possible. If your system is the type that utilizes PVC cement to glue together the parts, remember that you do not want to cement the downspouts to the drop outlets. If you do, you won't be able to take them apart to clean them out.

HOW TO FIGURE GUTTER SIZE

ROOF AREA (SQ. FT.)	GUTTER DIAMETER	DOWNSPOUT DIAMETER
100–800	4"	3"
800–1,000	5"	3"
1,000–1,400	5"	4"
1,400+	6"	4"

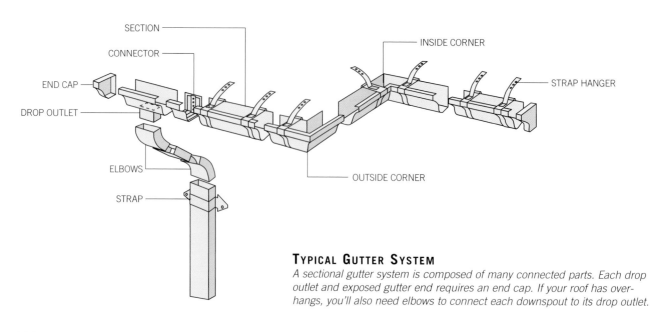

TYPICAL GUTTER SYSTEM
A sectional gutter system is composed of many connected parts. Each drop outlet and exposed gutter end requires an end cap. If your roof has overhangs, you'll also need elbows to connect each downspout to its drop outlet.

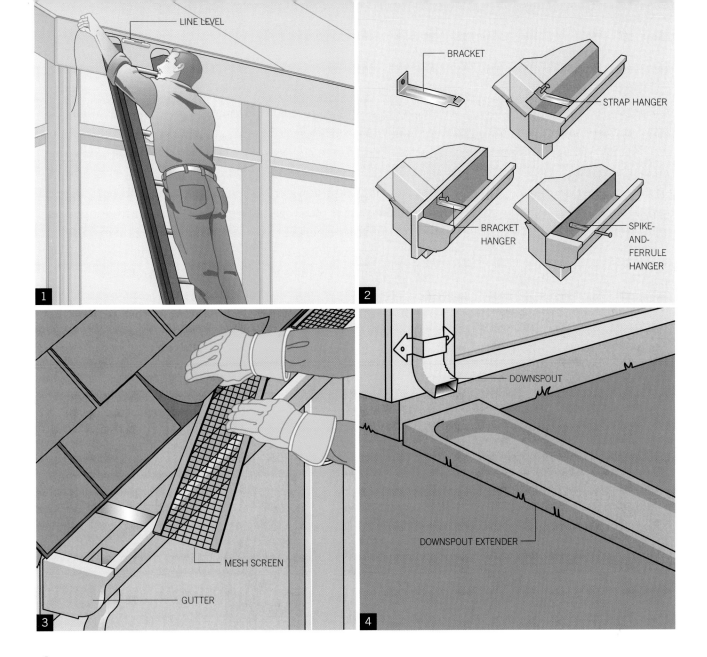

LINE LEVEL

1

BRACKET

STRAP HANGER

BRACKET HANGER

SPIKE-AND-FERRULE HANGER

2

MESH SCREEN

GUTTER

3

DOWNSPOUT

DOWNSPOUT EXTENDER

4

1 **To determine the slope,** position a string line immediately below where the gutter will be attached, and tie it to nails at each end. Use a line level to level the string, and then lower the string at the downspout end to achieve a drop of 1 inch per 20 feet.

2 **Align the gutter** with the string. Nail or screw the first hangers at the downspout end (three types of hangers are shown). Work outward from that point, fastening the gutter with one hanger every 3 feet. Secure the downspout with straps, using screws for wood siding and expanding anchors for masonry. Seal the straps with caulking.

3 **Add mesh screens** or other types of leaf catchers to deflect leaves, twigs, and other debris over the edge of the gutter. A leaf strainer will admit water but filter out debris, minimizing standing water that can serve as a breeding pool for bugs.

4 **Use downspout extenders** or splash blocks to carry drainage from downspouts away from the house. Water that flows from downspouts directly into the ground can erode the soil along the house, promoting settling and causing puddles that can serve as a place for bugs to breed.

APPLYING ASPHALT ROOFING

Standard three-tab asphalt shingles are the easiest of all roofing materials to install. They are affordable, long-lasting, and readily available at most home improvement centers. They are of a manageable weight and are a breeze to cut and nail.

The standard three-tab asphalt shingle measures 12 inches by 36 inches. Most have a self-sealing mastic that welds one tab to another after the shingles are installed. They should be applied over a solid deck of plywood sheathing and an underlayment of 15-pound roofing felt.

The correct weather exposure for most asphalt shingles is 5 inches (meaning that the lower 5 inches of each shingle will be exposed to the weather after overlapping courses are applied).

CUTTING AND NAILING

To cut shingles, score the backs along a carpenter's square or straightedge using a utility knife, and then bend them until they break. Choose nails that won't poke through the underside of the sheathing; 12-gauge, 1¼-inch-long galvanized roofing nails with ⅜-inch-diameter heads are typical. Drive nailheads until they just fit snugly against the shingles' surface to avoid breaking the shingles.

A narrow starter row of shingles will run the length of the eaves to form a base for the first full course of shingles. Before laying the starter course, measure the eaves and select enough 36-inch-long shingles to cover the distance. Apply a 9-inch-wide starter course—just cut 3 inches off the tabs of 12-inch-wide shingles.

Your main concern when you lay the second and successive courses is proper alignment of the shingles—both horizontally and vertically. Aligning shingles horizontally is simply a matter of snapping chalk lines across the deck. To align shingles vertically, snap chalk lines from the roof ridge to one end of every shingle along the first course.

When working with three-tab shingles, you can produce centered, diagonal, or random roof patterns by adjusting the length of the shingle that begins each course. Centered alignment creates the most uniform appearance but is the most difficult pattern to achieve. Diagonal alignment is a little more forgiving because the joints of four courses in a row are offset. Random alignment is the easiest of the three and creates a rustic appearance.

INSTALLING HIP AND RIDGE SHINGLES

If you haven't purchased ready-made ridge and hip shingles, cut 12-inch squares from standard shingles. Bend each square to conform to the roof ridge or hip (in cold weather, warm the shingles with a hair dryer before bending). Then snap a chalk line across the length of the ridge and each hip, 6 inches from the center.

HOW TO LAY ASPHALT SHINGLES

1 **Apply the starter course** along the eaves with the shingles' self-sealing strips down, starting at the left rake. Trim 6 inches off the first shingle's length to offset the cutouts in the starter course from those in the first course.

2 **Fasten the first course** of shingles to the deck using four nails placed 3 inches above the eave and 1 and 12 inches in from each end, allowing for a ½-inch overhang at both eaves and rakes and 1⁄16-inch spacing between shingles.

3 **Snap chalk lines** every 10 inches from the bottom of the first course, as shown. As you move toward the ridge, the upper edge of every other course of shingles should line up against the chalk lines.

4 **Start with the hips** if your roof has them. Begin with a double layer of shingles at the bottom of the hip and work toward the ridge, affixing shingles so there's a 5-inch exposure. The edge of each shingle should line up with the chalk mark.

5 **To shingle the ridge,** use two nails, one on each side, 5½ inches from the butt and 1 inch from the outside edge. Use nails long enough to penetrate the ridge board (about 2 inches long). Dab the nailheads of the last shingle with caulking compound.

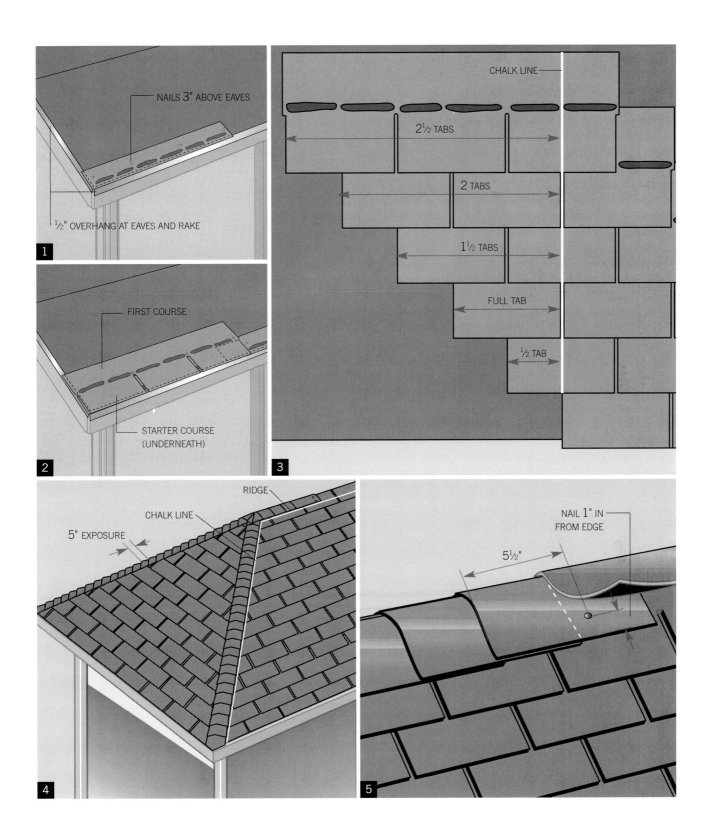

1 — NAILS 3" ABOVE EAVES / ½" OVERHANG AT EAVES AND RAKE

2 — FIRST COURSE / STARTER COURSE (UNDERNEATH)

3 — CHALK LINE / 2½ TABS / 2 TABS / 1½ TABS / FULL TAB / ½ TAB

4 — RIDGE / CHALK LINE / 5" EXPOSURE

5 — NAIL 1" IN FROM EDGE / 5½"

SCREENED ROOFS

Some screened rooms have open roofing that consists of screening stretched across a framework and—in some cases—a system of slats or latticework designed to throw partial shade.

The rules of thumb landscape architects use to figure lath spacing for shade are as follows: For lath ½ inch or less in thickness, the spacing should be from ⅜ to ¾ inch. For lath from ½ to 1⅛ inches thick, the spacing should be from ¾ to 1 inch. For 2 by 2s, the spacing can be 1½ to 2 inches where sun exposure is limited, but 1 to 1½ inches will make most patios or decks more comfortable.

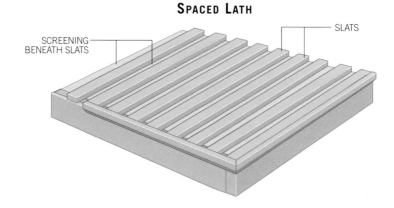

SCREENING BENEATH SLATS

SLATS

When you install latticework or slats, sight along the lumber to check for a "crown" and, when possible, face the crown upward. Use corrosion-resistant nails to secure the lath to the frame. With ⅜- or ½-inch-thick lath, use 3d or 4d common or box nails. For 1-inch stock, choose 8d nails. Use 12d or 16d for 2-inch-thick material. Nail twice at each rafter and at cut ends directly over rafters.

A certain amount of irregularity in the lath cover can be attractive; fortunately, you can count on the boards to provide this as they weather. Still, take care when affixing the lath. Though a little bit of twisting or bending relieves the severity of geometrically perfect installation, misalignment, sagging, and uneven spacing will be unattractive.

To cut down on the time spent on the rooftop, premake panels and fasten them to the rafters. You can build panels in many sizes, but about 3 by 6 feet is optimum for lightweight material. Be sure the structural framing is "true" enough to receive these panels without a struggle.

ROOFING WITH CORRUGATED PANELS

Plastic and aluminum corrugated panel systems generally come with instructions from the manufacturer. The 26-inch-wide panels have a 2-inch overlap; they are designed to connect to rafters on 24-inch centers. The panels should be supported along the seams for both strength and appearance. In addition, crossbracing is required every 5 feet to prevent the panels from sagging. If you want to minimize cutting, choose the panels you want to buy and adjust your structure to them.

You can cut plastic or aluminum panels with a fine-toothed handsaw or power saw equipped with a plywood-cutting or abrasive blade. Be sure to wear eye protection when cutting.

Predrill nail holes, backing the panel with a scrap block as you drill. Special aluminum twist nails with neoprene washers under the heads are made for these panels. Be sure to nail through the crowns of the corrugations, not through the valleys, as shown in the illustration below. Nail every 12 inches, taking care not to damage the panels as you hammer.

To make joints watertight where they overlap, sandwich a bead of silicone caulking compound between the lapped edges before you nail.

PANEL OVERLAP

MAKING WALL SECTIONS

Many screened porches and patios are not solely post-and-beam structures. Sections between the posts and/or above and below the screened openings are often framed and sided to match the house's walls. These sections are typically framed with 2-by-4 wall studs using conventional wall-framing techniques after the sub-flooring or decking has been installed. Just measure, cut, and assemble these sections, as shown in the illustration at right (also see page 42), using 16d nails.

Be sure to choose siding patterns that will look good with your house and will shed rain. Installation methods vary widely, depending on the material.

If your type of siding requires a base of panel sheathing, apply this first. Use 8d galvanized nails to fasten panels (usually horizontally) to wall studs, spacing the nails 6 inches apart mid-panel (or as specified by codes). Allow an expansion gap of $\frac{1}{16}$ inch between the panels.

Next, apply building paper in horizontal strips, starting at the bottom and working up. Overlap the strips by 2 inches at horizontal joints and by 6 inches at vertical joints. To cut the paper, use a utility knife. Staple or nail the paper to studs or sheathing, using just enough fasteners to hold it in place until the siding is installed.

Sidings that overlap—whether solid boards, vinyl, aluminum, or another material—are installed

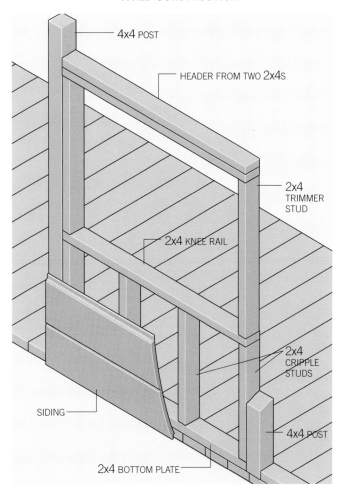

4x4 POST

HEADER FROM TWO 2x4s

2x4 TRIMMER STUD

2x4 KNEE RAIL

2x4 CRIPPLE STUDS

4x4 POST

SIDING

2x4 BOTTOM PLATE

from the bottom up. Establish a straight, level baseline along the bottom for the first panel, and keep successive panels in alignment; recheck level as you move up the wall.

When installing manufactured sidings, such as vinyl or aluminum, follow the manufacturer's instructions.

If you're installing board siding, run a 1-by-2 starter strip along the baseline to prop out the first siding board at the correct angle. Allow a 1-inch overlap as you nail $1\frac{1}{2}$ inches from the bottom edge at each stud with 8d or 10d galvanized nails (which size will

depend on the siding's thickness).

If you use plywood siding, plan to install sheet-metal Z-flashing along any horizontal joints between panels. Allow a $\frac{1}{16}$-inch expansion gap between panels, and caulk the seams.

Finish around windows or screened bays and doors, using 1-by-4 trim or similar material. Note that, in some cases, it's easiest to apply this trim first and then butt the siding up to the trim and caulk any gaps.

Be sure to apply a protective finish of water repellent, primer, or stain to wood siding to ensure that it will last for years.

credits

SCREENED RETREATS

1 Photographer: Brian Vanden Brink
2 Photographer: Brian Vanden Brink; Builder: James Beyor 4 Photographer: Jean Allsopp; Photo stylist: Lisa Powell 6 left Photographer: Brian Vanden Brink; Architect: Stephen Blatt 6 right Photographer: John O'Hagan; Photo stylist: Lisa Allison; Builders: Whitehurst Builders Inc.; Designers: Pat & Meg 7 top Photographer: Brian Vanden Brink; Architect: Rob Whitten 7 right Photographer: Jessie Walker; Architect: Chuck Hackley 8 bottom left Photographer: Jessie Walker 8 top right Photographer: Brian Vanden Brink; Architect: Mark Hutker & Associates 9 top right Photographer: Jessie Walker 9 bottom right Photographer: Timothy Hursley; Architects: Mark Simon, FAIA, and Charles G. Mueller, AIA/Centerbrook Architects 10 bottom left Photographer: Jean-Claude Hurni; Designer: Richard Proulx 10 right Photographer: Sylvia Martin; Photo stylist: Rose Nguyen 11 top Photographer: Jessie Walker 11 bottom Photographer: Robert Perron; Architect: Robert Orr Architects 12 Photographer: Jean-Claude Hurni; Designers: Décor Nature 13 top Photographer: Jean-Claude Hurni 13 bottom Photographer: Jean-Claude Hurni; Designer: Richard Proulx 14 both Photographer: Brian Vanden Brink; Architect: Rob Whitten 15 top Photographer: Jean-Claude Hurni; Designers/Builders: Daniel Hébert and Rose-Élise Cialdella 15 bottom left and right Photographer: Robert Perron; Designer: Structura 16 bottom left Photographer: Jean-Claude Hurni; Designer: Cabanon & Patio Maison Jaune 16 top right Photographer: Jean-Claude Hurni; Designer: Olivier Le Clerc/Les Jardins du Magnolia 17 top left and right Photographer: Jean-Claude Hurni; Designer: Bruno Tassé/Bizzart 17 bottom Photographer: Jean-Claude Hurni; Designers: Les Embellissements Paysagers Laval Inc. 18 both Photographer: Leigh McLoud;
Designer: Lake/Flato Architects 19 top Photographer: Paul Bardagjy; Designer: Dick Clark/Dick Clark Architecture 19 bottom Photo courtesy of the Aluminum Association of Florida 20 Photographer: Sylvia Martin; Designer: de la Guardia Victoria Architects 21 top and center Photographer: Paul Bardagjy; Designer: Michael Imber/Michael Imber Architects 21 bottom Photographer: Brian Vanden Brink; Architect: Carol A. Wilson

PLANNING AND DESIGN

22 Photographer: Norman McGrath; Designers: Charles W. Moore, FAIA, and Mark Simon, FAIA, with James Childress, FAIA/Centerbrook Architects 24 Photographer: Jean-Claude Hurni 25 top Photographer: James R. Salomon; Architect: Carol A. Wilson 25 bottom Photographer: Meg McKinney Simle; Architect: Patrick N. Fox 26 Photographer: Paul Bardagjy; Designer: Jeffrey Berkus/BBG Architects 27 Photographer: Jamie Hadley; Interior Designer: Michael D. Trapp 30 left Photo courtesy of the Aluminum Association of Florida 30 right Photographer: Timothy Hursley; Architect: Tom Howorth, FAIA 31 Photographer: Brian Vanden Brink; Architect: Carol A. Wilson 32–34 all Photos courtesy of Dalton Pavilions Inc. 35 Photographer: Brian Vanden Brink; Designer: Mark Hutker & Associates 36 Photographer: Timothy Hursley; Designer: Jefferson B. Riley, FAIA/Centerbrook Architects 37 Photo courtesy of Four Seasons Sunrooms

SCREENED-ROOM PROJECTS

38 Photographer: Jean Allsopp/SPC Photo Collection; Designer: M. Taylor Dawson III/Wilson & Dawson Architects 40 Photographer: John O'Hagan/SPC Photo Collection 41 top left Photographer: Brian Vanden Brink 41 top right Photographer: Brian Vanden Brink; Designer: Scholz+Barclay
41 bottom Photos courtesy of Screen Tight 44 both Photographer: Derek Fell 48 Photo courtesy of Dave Lombardo/ American Deck, Inc.; Architect: Dave Lombardo/American Deck, Inc. 54 Photographer: Robert Perron; Designer: Robert Orr Architects 60 Photo courtesy of Dalton Pavilions Inc. 64 Photographer: Sylvia Martin; Architect: Lou Kimball, AIA
70 Photographer: E. Andrew McKinney; Designer: Jim Knott 74 Photographer: Jessie Walker 76–77 both Photographer: Jean Allsopp/SPC Photo Collection; Designer: M. Taylor Dawson III/Wilson & Dawson Architects 78 Photographer: Brian Vanden Brink; Designer: Jack Silverio 79 Photo courtesy of Vixen Hill Gazebos 80, 81 top right Photographer: Sylvia Martin; Photo stylist: Rose Nguyen 81 top left Photographer: Jean Allsopp/SPC Photo Collection; Photo stylist: Buffy Hargett; Architect: McAlpine Tankersly Architecture 81 bottom left Photographer: Jean-Claude Hurni; Designer: Richard Proulx 81 bottom right Photographer: Sylvia Martin/SPC Photo Collection; Architect: Jim Thomas 84 Photographer: Timothy Hursley; Designer: Jefferson B. Riley, FAIA/ Centerbrook Architects

BUILDING TECHNIQUES

86 Photographer: Paul Bardagjy; Designer: Charles Travis/Travis Architects 88–89 all Photographer: Scott Fitzgerrell 90–93 all Photographer: Don Vandervort 94 all except bottom left Photographer: Stephen O'Hara for HomeTips Inc. 94 bottom left Photographer: Don Vandervort 95 top Photographer: Scott Fitzgerrell 95 center and bottom Photographer: Norman A. Plate 101 all Photographer: Mark Rutherford 102–103 all Photographer: Christopher Vendetta 104 Photo courtesy of Trowel Trades Red Lion 105 Photographer: Mark Rutherford 106 Photographer: Scott Atkinson 109–114 all Photographer: Mark Rutherford

index

RESOURCES

Aluminum Association of Florida
(561) 362-9019
www.aaof.org

American Deck Inc.
(800) 592-3325
www.amdeck.com

Archadeck
(804) 353-6999
www.archadeck.com

Artistic Enclosures
(800) 944-8599
www.artisticenclosures.com

Dalton Pavilions Inc.
(215) 721-1492
www.daltonpavilions.com

EZ Screen
(garage-door screen kit)
(800) 734-5307
www.ezscreenkit.com

Four Seasons Sunrooms
(800) 368-7732
www.fourseasonssunrooms.com

Metals USA
(972) 882-8916
www.metalsusa.com

Phifer Wire Products Inc.
(800) 874-3007
www.phifer.com

Screen Tight
(800) 768-7325
www.screentight.com

Vixen Hill Gazebos
(800) 423-2766
www.vixenhill.com